Generis

PUBLISHING

ASSESSING THE IMPLEMENTATION OF PROBLEM-BASED LEARNING METHOD IN GEOGRAPHY EDUCATION: A STUDY OF UNIVERSITY OF CAPE COAST

SAMUEL BENTIL

CIP a Camerei Naţionale a Cărţii

Bentil, Samuel.

Assessing the implementation of problem-based learning method in geography education: a study of University of Cape Coast / Samuel Bentil. – Chişinău : Generis Publishing, 2020 (Print on demand). – 103 p. : fig., tab.
Bibliogr.: p. 80-91.

ISBN 978-9975-154-42-0.

378.091:911 B 45

Cover image: www.pixabay.com

Generis Publishing
Online orders: www.generis-publishing.com
Orders by email: info@generis-publishing.com

ABSTRACT

Problem-based learning is one of the methods used by some lecturers in the University of Cape Coast in teaching geography courses. However, works that explored problem-based learning as a method of instruction in geography education appears to have been done outside the Ghanaian context (Spronken-Smith, 2005; Pawson et al., 2006; Golightly et al., 2013; Quain, 2014). Hence, to bridge the gap in terms of location and literature, this study sought to assess the implementation of problem-based learning method in geography education in the University of Cape Coast in the Central Region of Ghana. The pragmatist research paradigm (Mixed method) mainly the Convergent parallel design was employed for the study. Census and purposive sampling techniques were employed and questionnaire and interview guides (one for student focus group discussion and another for lecturers' in-depth interview) were used for data collection. The study found that instructors define or present the problem, conduct objectives and context specification for students. Large class size and inadequate resources were the pressing challenges affecting the use of the PBL method in geography. Besides, it was found that PBL develops geography students' observation and problem-solving skills, confidence and attitude towards the subject, promotes lifelong learning among others. In view of this, it is recommended that the Department of Geography and Regional Planning and the Department of Business and Social Sciences Education should provide support and guidance to students and instructors by setting up a fund where students can be levied as part of their fees and organising PBL seminars to promote the effective use of the PBL method in all geography courses.

ACKNOWLEDGEMENTS

I would like to express my profound gratitude to my supervisors, Dr. Collins Adjei Mensah and Dr. Bethel Tawiah Ababio who professionally and carefully edited, gave constructive criticisms and immense contributions as well as their fatherly love. I am sincerely grateful. Also, my intense gratitude goes to Prof. Kwabena Barima Antwi, Prof. Cosmas Cobbold, Prof. Kankam Boadu, Alhaji Dr. M. B. Yidana (HoD) and Dr. Joseph Tufour Kwarteng for their advice, encouragement and generous contributions to make this work better.

Again, I am grateful to Mr. Hillary Dumba and Mr. Shadrack Yaw Agyiri for their special assistance which enabled me to finish on time. Finally, I wish to thank my family, National Executives of GHAMSU (NEG), MPhil Colleagues, friends and especially Level 300 and 400 B.Sc. Geography and Regional Planning Students and B.Ed. Social Sciences Education (Geography Major) students for their unflinching support during the filling of the questionnaire and the focus group discussion.

DEDICATION

To my mentors: Dr. Bethel Tawiah Ababio, Prof. Cosmas Cobbold and Mrs. Sarah Teye

TABLE OF CONTENTS

CHAPTER ONE

INTRODUCTION

Problem-based learning (PBL) has been found to be more suitable teaching method for the geography curriculum (Spronken-Smith, 2005; Golightly & Muniz, 2013; Quain, 2014). This revelation came as a result of studies conducted on PBL as a method of instruction in geography. However, these studies appear to be concentrated outside Ghana. Meanwhile, PBL method is used by some lecturers in geography instruction in the University of Cape Coast in the Central Region and no study has been done on its efficacy in geography instruction. Hence, the investigator deems it expedient to assess the implementation of PBL method in geography in order to determine whether the finding of other studies which found PBL as a suitable for geography is the case in the context of University of Cape Coast in the Central Region of Ghana. Hence, this chapter presented the background to the study, problem statement, research objectives, questions and hypotheses; significant, delimitation and limitation as well as organisation of the study.

Background to the Study

The word *geography* was adopted in the 200s BC by the Greek scholar Eratosthenes and means "earth description". Bergman and Renwick (2008) defined geography as the study of the interaction of all physical and human phenomena at individual places and of how interactions among places form patterns and organise space. Also, Ababio (2012) defined geography as the study of the surface of the earth, location and distribution of its physical and cultural features, the areal pattern they form, and the interrelation of these features as they affect human beings. Bergman and Renwick and Ababio's definitions were comprehensive, since they touch on the traditions or the themes in geography which include physical, human, spatial, area and human-environment interaction tradition. Additionally, the physical tradition studies the surface of the earth and of the natural and physical forces which exert their influence in, on or around the earth.

Furthermore, the human tradition deals with the human groups and activities such as language, industry and the building of cities. Besides, the spatial tradition is also known as locational analysis which looks for patterns in the distribution of human actions and environmental processes and in movement across the earth's surface. Also, the area geography deals with describing and compiling geographic data about places or an area. Lastly, the human-environment tradition studies the interaction between human and his environment. That is how the physical systems or environment affects human system and also, how human actions modify the physical environment as well as the changes that occur in the meaning, use, distribution and importance of resources.

Education in geography has been necessitated by the fact that individuals need to understand the spatial settings of people and resources around them – people everywhere try to make sense of their lives. They want to know the nature of the world and their place in it. Humans want to understand the intrinsic nature of their home (Ababio, 2012). Ababio explained that geography education is the development, organisation and dissemination of knowledge, understanding, skills and values in geography. This depicts the integrated nature of geography (Waugh, 2009).

The nature of Geography as a discipline makes it imperative for the teacher to possess a special body of knowledge, skills and characteristics. The teacher needs to understand the materials he/she teaches, how to teach it and why he/she should teach it. That is, he/she should have adequate subject matter, pedagogic and curriculum knowledge. In addition, the teacher should have a powerful grasp of the ways of teaching geography and the materials for teaching it (Ababio, 2009). This implies that the pedagogical knowledge and strategies to teach the subject is very essential in order to achieve effective and efficient teaching and learning process.

Geography is both a powerful medium for promoting the education of individuals and a major contributor to international, environmental and development education. Through their studies in geography, students are encouraged to explore and develop knowledge, understanding, skills, attitudes and values which constitute the holistic process of education. The knowledge gained from the study of geography helps primary/elementary school pupils to learn, as lessons in environmental studies take them out to explore their surroundings, thus opening them to new experiences and teaching them about the cultures and lifestyles of other people and places (Ababio, 2007).

To the secondary school student, geography affords adolescents the opportunity to develop their capacity for abstract thinking as the practical experience gained at the primary/elementary school level is augmented by increasing use of more abstract sources of information. Geography at this level aims at avoiding a separation of knowledge and behaviour, and encouraging environmental competence, regional and national commitment and multicultural and international perspectives (Ababio, 2007).

Besides, Bork, Hemmer and Czapek (2012) indicated that the main goals of geography lessons are to provide insights into the connections between natural conditions and social activities in different parts of the world, and to teach an associated spatially-oriented competence that can be applied. Students can also learn to understand the resulting structures, processes and problems involved with these interactions and to consider solutions for these problems. With this general geography approach, geography education makes special contribution to the encouragement of multi-perspective, systematic and problem-solving thinking. In addition, school lessons must be viewed as a dynamic process in which teachers perform in complex situations with manifold interactions, and in which the effects of a specific teacher's intervention vary depending on location, time, pupils` individual dispositions and class composition (Helmke, 2009).

Geography as a subject was basically taught in Ghana in the 1950's to the 1980's through the Capes and Bays approach, that is, the listing of names of places which include relief and cultural features, location of continents, countries, capital and regional or provincial cities (Kattah, 2015). In addition, it was not taught as independent subject at the basic level but rather it was part of environmental studies and social studies. Furthermore, in the 1987 Educational Reform, it was taught as independent discipline with distinct branches such as physical, human/regional and practical geography including map work. From the 1990's to date, geography is taught as a major discipline in the secondary and the tertiary level. At the senior high school level, it is an elective subject in the General Arts programme; and at the tertiary level, it is studied as independently as either Bachelor of Arts Geography or Bachelor of Science Geography. It is also studied at the masters and doctoral levels with specialisation in any of the branches of physical, human/regional and practical geography or map work (Ababio, 2012). At all these levels how the subject is understood by students depends on the effectiveness of the teaching methods employed by the teacher.

According to Lefrancois (as cited in Tamakloe, 2004), effective teaching requires two basic competencies and skills. First, is the process of teaching (method) which consists of a group of skills for organising content of a lesson and for attaining instructional objectives. The second consists of a group of personal and social skills for a successful functioning in the school for relating with parents and administrators. Hence, the effective geography teacher should have adequate knowledge in the various branches of geography (physical, practical and human/regional). In addition, the geography teacher should employ varied teaching methods and resources in his/her teaching as well as developing positive attitudes towards the teaching of geography to ensure effective and efficient teaching and learning process.

Furthermore, McBer (2000) stressed that the success of every teaching and learning interaction depends on factors such as students' perception towards the learning of the discipline, teacher quality, teaching methods employed by teachers and some environmental factors such as the time allocation for the teaching and learning of the subject as well as teaching and learning aids. This shows that, for effective teaching and learning interaction to take place, the methods employed play significant role in it. Singh and Rana (2004) defined teaching methods as something designed to establish interactions among the teacher, the student and the subject matter to influence directly or indirectly the learning process. He further indicates that, with reference to the current trend in geography, teachers need to have a number of teaching methods at their disposal from which they can select the most appropriate. Some of the teaching methods include lecture, discussion, problem-based learning, brainstorming, observation, role play, question-and-answer, activity, field trips, group work, field work, enquiry and among other methods.

Hayford (1992) indicated that the lecture method has persisted in the teaching of geography and social studies because it has been found appropriate to obtaining significant objectives. Lecture method as defined by Kelly (2014) is a teaching method where an instructor is the central focus of information transfer. She further indicated that lecture as a method of teaching is straight forward way to impart knowledge to students quickly. Though it makes instructors to have a greater control over what is being taught in the classroom because they are the sole sources of information, Bligh (2000) summarised that most lectures as a method of teaching are not as effective as discussion for promoting thought. In addition, it is ineffective for teaching values associated with the subject matter and for inspiring interest in a subject as well as for personal and social adjustment.

Padmavathy and Mareesh (2013) describes PBL as a learning environment where problems drive the learning. That is, learning begins with a problem to be solved, and the problem is presented in such a way that students need to gain new knowledge in order to solve it. Also, advocates of problem-based and discovery learning argue that children who acquire knowledge on their own are more likely to apply and extend that knowledge than those who receive direct instruction (Alliance for Childhood, 2000; Bok, 2006). Additionally, studies have revealed that problem-based learning is a more suitable teaching approach for the geography curriculum (Spronken-Smith, 2005; Golightly & Muniz, 2013; Quain, 2014). For example, Quain indicated PBL promote self-directed and long-life learning resulting to developing positive attitude among geography students in geography education.

Besides, Alfieri, Brooks, Aldrich and Tenenbuam (2011) emphasised that allowing learners to interact with materials, manipulate variables, explore phenomena, and attempt to apply principles affords them with opportunities to notice patterns, discover underlying causalities, and learn in ways that are seemingly more robust. This implies that through problem-based learning, geography students are encouraged to explore and develop knowledge, understanding, skills, attitudes and values which constitute the holistic process of education to solve problems of the society and the nation at large. It is against this background that the investigator seeks to examine the implementation of problem-based leaning method in geography education in the context of the University of Cape Coast.

The investigator is conducting the study in geography due to the fact that Geography which is the study of the earth's surface, location and distribution of its physical and cultural features, the areal pattern they form, and the interrelation of these features as they affect human beings warrant such instruction approach in it teaching and learning of the subject. Also, since the earth is one of the laboratory of the geographer and observation being one of the instrument in fieldwork, there is a need to examine PBL method implementation in geography education in the University of Cape Coast.

Statement of the Problem

Geography education has "strong traditions of small-group work, both through laboratory and field teaching, [and] is well placed to try such teaching methods as problem-based learning" (Spronken-Smith, 2005, p. 203). In the problem-based learning approach, complex, real-world problems are used to motivate students to identify and research the concepts and principles they need to know to work through those problems (Duch, Groh, & Allen, 2001). However, it appears most studies conducted on problem-based learning as a method of instruction in geography education were conducted outside Ghana (Spronken-Smith, 2005; Pawson et al., 2006; Golightly & Muniz, 2013; Quain, 2014). For example, Spronken-Smith's (2005) study on "implementing a problem-based learning approach for teaching research methods in geography" was done in New Zealand. Pawson et al.'s research on "Problem-based learning in geography: Towards a critical assessment of its purposes, benefits and risks" was conducted in New Zealand. Besides, Golightly and Muniz (2013) study "Are South African geography education students ready for problem-based learning?" was also conducted in South Africa while Quain's (2014) study "Assessing students' attitudes towards geography in a problem-based learning environment" was done in Illinois of USA. This shows a knowledge gap in terms of locations where studies on problem-based learning have been undertaken with none of the above studies focusing on Ghana.

Furthermore, most of these studies (Spronken-Smith, 2005; Pawson et al., 2006; Golightly & Muniz, 2013; Quain, 2014) in geography education focused on different aspects of problem-based learning. For instance, Spronken-Smith approach was on implementing a problem-based learning approach for teaching research methods in geography while that of Pawson et al. was on a critical assessment of the purposes, benefits and risks of problem-based learning. Additionally, Golightly et al. approach was on looking whether South African geography education students are ready for problem-based learning. Moreover, Quain's study was on students' attitudes towards geography in a problem-based learning environment. Although these studies have looked at different aspects of problem-based learning, they have not touched on the challenges affecting the effective implementation of PBL in geography and the ways for ensuring effective implementation of PBL method in geography education, hence creating a knowledge gap in that area. It was in order to fill the above identified knowledge gap that this study was undertaken on assessing the implementation of problem-based learning as a method of instruction in geography education in Ghana specifically in the University of Cape Coast.

Purpose of the Study

The purpose of the study was to examine the implementation of problem-based learning (PBL) in geography education in the University of Cape Coast. Specifically, the study sought to:

1. Assess the processes or stages involved in the implementation of the Problem-based learning method in geography education.
2. Assess the challenges affecting the effective implementation of the problem-based learning method in geography education.
3. Examine ways for ensuring effective implementation of the Problem-based learning method in geography education.
4. Examine the benefits of effective implementation of the Problem-based learning method in geography education.

Research Questions

Due to the broad nature of the topic under the study, the following research questions were formulated to guide the study.

1. What are the processes or stages involved in the implementation of the Problem-based learning method in geography education?
2. What are the challenges affecting the effective implementation of the problem-based learning method in geography education?
3. What are the ways for ensuring effective implementation of PBL method in geography education?
4. What are the benefits of effective implementation of the Problem-based learning method in geography education?

Significance of the Study

The study would provide information to assist University of Cape Coast geography lecturers, students, educational planners, administrators among others in their educational planning and enable them adopt appropriate instructional approach or measures to promote effective teaching and learning of geography. Since the study would bring to light the processes involved in Problem-based learning (PBL) implementation as a method and the benefits associated with it, it would enable other geography and non-geography lecturers who do not use it to adopt it in their instructional process.

In addition, it would enlighten and motivate students to appreciate the PBL method of instruction in geography better, having been equipped with knowledge of its benefits and the processes involved in its use. Again, it would help geography lecturers, administrators, students and other educational planners to strategised the Geography curriculum in a way that would enable the effective implementation of PBL method, since, the study would provide information on the factors that affect its effective implementation and ways to overcome associated challenges.

Furthermore, the findings from the research would serve as a source of information for planning in-serving training for geography lecturers on the effective use of Problem-based learning as a method of instruction in geography. Besides, the findings from the study would contribute to the exiting knowledge on the topic under study and serve as a reference point for further investigation into the implementation of problem-based learning in geography education.

Delimitation of the Study

Owing to the comprehensive nature of the study, it was delimited to assessing processes or stages involved in the implementation of problem-based learning method in teaching geography and the benefits of PBL as a method of instruction. In addition, the study was delimited to challenges affecting the effective implementation of PBL in geography education and the ways of making its implementation effective in teaching geography. The study was delimited to level 300 and 400 BSc Geography and Regional Planning Students who are reading Planning Workshop in Department of Geography and Regional Planning and level 300 and 400 B.Ed. (Social Sciences-Geography Major) in the Department of Business and Social Sciences Education of the University of Cape Coast. The justification for these groups of students and their lecturers was because they employ the PBL method in teaching their courses.

Limitations of the Study

This study has its limitation, like any other research. The authenticity of informants' responses – participants' experiences, perspectives and explanations limited the degree to which the results could be transferred to other context. Since the study is a case of only University of Cape Coast and not all the universities in the country, the findings cannot be generalised beyond the study area. In addition, the population from which the sample was drawn was limited as it excluded some groups of people. Absenteeism of some students during the data collection period negatively affected the retrieval rate which would have influence the reliability of the results of the study. The investigator extended the period for one and half months before return rate of 91% was obtained.

Organisation of the Study

The overall study was organised into five main chapters. Chapter One dealt with the introduction of the study which consists of the background to the study, statement of the problem, purpose of the study, research questions, significance of the study, limitations and delimitation of the study. Chapter Two focused on the review of related literature on efficacy of PBL method in geography education, highlighting the theoretical underpinning of the study and conceptual reviews as well as correlated empirical studies on the research questions. Besides, Chapter Three dealt with the research methodology of the study which comprises research design, population, sample and sampling procedure, research instrument, data collection procedure and data analysis. Chapter Four also focused on the results and discussion of findings of the study. The last chapter (five) dealt with the summary of the study and making conclusions based on the finding of the study as well as making recommendations based on the research questions raised. In the same chapter, suggestions were made for further research.

CHAPTER TWO
LITERATURE REVIEW

Overview

This chapter focuses on the review of literature pertaining to the topic under study. The chapter incorporates theoretical framework, conceptual and empirical issues. Under the theoretical issues, the constructivists theory of learning was reviewed to aid the understanding of the study. Also, the 3C3R PBL model by Hung (2006a) was adopted to aid the study. The conceptual issues centred on the concept of Problem-based learning (PBL), the processes or stages involved in the implementation of PBL in geography education, benefit of PBL in teaching geography, challenges affecting its effective implementation and ways to ensure its effective implementation in geography education. The empirical review on the other hand was devoted to reviewing the works done by others which are related to or have bearing on this study. This allows for comparison to be made between the findings that would emerge from this study and the earlier findings from previous studies.

Concept of problem-based learning (PBL)

Historically, PBL was pioneered in the medical school program at McMaster University in Hamilton, Ontario, Canada in the late 1960s by Howard Barrows and his colleagues (Neville, 2009). Barrows (1996) indicates that the traditional medical education disenchanted students, who perceived the vast amount of material presented in the first three years of medical school as having little relevance to the practice of medicine and clinically based medicine. In addition, Barrows and Tamblyn (as cited in Savin-Baden, 2000) established that some medical students gathered data ritualistically and then tried to add it up afterwards, while others came up with a diagnosis based on some symptom or sign, never considering possible alternatives. Hence, the PBL curriculum was developed in order to stimulate the learners, assist the learners in seeing the relevance of learning to future roles, maintain a higher level of motivation towards learning, and to show the learners the importance of responsible, professional attitudes. Also, Savin-Baden (2000) reveals that the rationale behind problem-based learning stemmed from years of observing experts engaged in clinical reasoning, resulting in Barrows and Tamblyn's (1980) claim that problem-based learning was based on two assumptions. The first was that learning through problem situations was much more effective than memory-based learning for creating a usable body of knowledge. The second was that the medical skills that were most important for treating patients were problem-solving skills, rather than memorization.

However, the essential focus of this approach adopted at McMaster was not on problem-solving learning whereby individual students were expected to answer a series of questions from information supplied by a lecturer. Instead, they were asked, in small teams, to explore a problem situation (Savin-Baden, 2000). Through such an exploration student were expected to examine the gaps in their own knowledge and skills in order to decide what information they needed to acquire in order to resolve or manage the situation with which they were presented. Much the same can be said of the education of geography students, many of whom will enter careers that are not related to their first degree expertise (Pawson et al., 2006).   According to Wu and Fournier (2000), the ability for these students to learn as self-starters in new situations is clearly vital, and they have "little need for content-driven instruction" in geography (p. 112). Moreover, those who do make careers drawing directly on their degrees, such as in geographic information systems and environmental management, face a similar pace of knowledge renewal to those in medicine. Hence, core competencies are vital, but need to be sufficiently understood in order to be applied in different situations. What matters, then, is the ability to 'learn to learn' rather than what is actually learned or taught (Healey, 2005).

Several other researchers (Barrows, 1996; Duch, Groh & Allen, 2001; Peters & Amador, 2006; Armstrong, 2008; Gasser, 2011) indicated that problem-based learning has subsequently been adopted by other medical school programs, adapted for undergraduate instruction, as well as K-12. Furthermore, the use of PBL has expanded from its initial introduction into medical school programs to include education in the areas of other health sciences, mathematics, law, education, economics, business, social studies, and engineering (Gasser, 2011). Moreover, the use of PBL, like other student-centered pedagogies, has been motivated by recognition of the failures of traditional instruction and the emergence of a deeper understanding into how people learn (Cotič & Zuljan, 2009).

Barrows (2000) defined Problem-Based Learning (PBL) as a method of learning in which students first encounter a problem, followed by a student-centered inquiry process. Additionally, Pawson et al. (2006) defined PBL as a development and instructional approach built around an ill-structured problem that is messy and complex in nature; requires inquiry, information gathering and reflection; is changing and tentative and has no simple, fixed and formulaic right solution. Furthermore, Mayer (2013) defined PBL to consist of a multi-phased collaborative approach to education where students gain knowledge as they work in small groups (3-5 students) and attempt to solve a problem carefully-designed by the instructor. He further indicates that throughout the problem-solving process, students work together, integrating existing knowledge and seeking out new knowledge, all with the help of the instructor.

The key to PBL is that learning, for the most part, is pull-based (students seek the necessary knowledge) rather than push-based (students are fed knowledge by an instructor) (Schmidt, Rotgans & Yew, 2011). From various definitions of PBL, it can be implied that problem-based learning is a method whose focus is on the problem-solving process with students exploring ideas and constructing their own knowledge with or without the help of the teacher. Besides, the teachers may also present a problem to the class in groups to explore and get solutions to. This means that PBL, as a method of instruction for geography, demands the geography tutor to structure lessons and present them in a problem format for the students to explore by integrating their existing geographical concepts and knowledge to seek solutions to the problem presented to the class. This can be done with the help of the tutor as a facilitator or without his/her help.

Characteristics of problem-based learning (PBL)

According to Hung, Jonassen and Liu (2008), "problem-based learning is an instructional methodology; that is, it is an instructional solution to learning problems" (p. 488). They further indicate that the primary goal of PBL is to enhance learning by requiring learners to solve problems. Hung et al. outline the following characteristics for PBL approach:

1. It is problem-focused, such that learners begin learning by addressing simulations of an authentic, ill-structured problem. The content and skills to be learned are organized around problems, rather than as a hierarchical list of topics, so a reciprocal relationship exists between knowledge and the problem. Knowledge building is stimulated by the problem and applied back to the problem.
2. It is student-centred, because faculty cannot dictate learning.
3. It is self-directed, such that students individually and collaboratively assume responsibility for generating learning issues and processes through self-assessment and peer assessment and assess their own learning materials. Required assignments are rarely made.
4. It is self-reflective, such that learners monitor their understanding and learn to adjust strategies for learning.
5. Tutors are facilitators (not knowledge disseminators) who support and model reasoning processes, facilitate group processes and interpersonal dynamics, probe students' knowledge deeply, and never interject content or provide direct answers to questions.

Also, De Graaff and Kolmos (2003) noted that PBL education is based on the students' background, expectations, and interests. It is a very common experience that students are more motivated and work much harder with the PBL model than with traditional teaching methods. They also spend a great deal of time on PBL work. Additionally, Wilkerson and Gijselaers (1996) claim that "PBL is characterized by a student-centred approach, teachers as facilitators rather than disseminators, and open-ended problems (called ill-structured) that serve as the initial stimulus and framework for learning" (pp. 101-102). Here, the instructor's aim is to develop students' intrinsic interest in the subject matter, emphasize learning rather than to recall, promote group work, and help students become self-directed learners (White, 2001). Furthermore, learning is "student-centred" because the students are given the freedom to study those topics that interest them the most and to determine how they want to study them. Therefore, Gallagher (1997) opined that students should identify their learning needs, help plan classes, lead class discussions, and assess their own work and their classmates' work.

In addition to emphasizing learning by "doing," PBL requires students to be metacognitively aware (Gijselaers, 1996). That is, students must learn to be conscious of what information they already know about the problem, what information they need to know to solve the problem, and the strategies to use to solve the problem. Being able to articulate such thoughts helps students become more effective problem-solvers and self-directed learners. Initially, many students are not capable of this sort of thinking on their own. For this reason, the instructor must become a tutor or cognitive coach who models problem inquiry strategies, guides exploration, and helps students clarify and pursue their research questions (Arámbula-Greenfield, 1996). In agreement with Arámbula-Greenfield, Stepien and Gallagher (as cited in Quian, 2014) pointed that teachers must model behaviour they want students to use and serve as collaborators with students to help them solve the problem. Students will learn from the problems they encounter and the community will serve as the textbook (Bednarz, 2004). Therefore, students must read the needs of their community to solve the problem.

This means the instructor plays a critical role in helping students become self-directed learners and must create a classroom environment in which students "receive systematic instruction in conceptual, strategic, and reflective reasoning in the context of a discipline that will ultimately make them more successful in later investigations" (Gallagher, 1997, p. 337). Gallagher also suggests that teachers "give voice to metacognitive questions" and "insert them into the classroom dialog so that students learn to attend to them, appreciate their utility, and then adopt their use as they become increasingly independent and self-directed" (p. 340).

Considering the characteristics of PBL, we find that learners are major determinants in the instructional process. This implies that decisions on what and how to study, the knowledge and the skills to be acquired focus much on the learner, unlike the lecture method where the instructors determine whatever information or knowledge to give to the learners. In addition, such decisions are determined by the teacher in agreement with the whole class. Moreover, there is either individualised learning or group work in problem-based learning. In individualised learning, the problem is presented to individual students to explore and find solutions to solve it whereas group work requires that students are grouped and particular problems or situations are presented to them to discuss amongst themselves to find solutions to. Furthermore, PBL is well-placed in a student-centred classroom. According to Utecht (2003), student-centred classroom is a classroom where the students are actively involved in the learning process. Here, students move away from following orders given by a teacher to self-directed learning activities, from memorizing and repeating information to discovering information on their own. Besides, students communicate and take responsibility for their learning instead of listening and reacting to lessons.

Gentry (2000) pointed out that student-centred classrooms "focus on the understanding of the processes instead of on knowledge of facts, terms and content. Most importantly, student-centred environments focus on lifelong learning and not just learning in youth" (p. 9). These characteristics of PBL best fit the nature of geography because in geography, observation, fieldwork or trip among others are major tools for making the teaching and learning of the subject easier and more understandable for learners. Hence, a geography instructor adopting PBL as a method of instruction must first understand its principles and apply it accordingly to ensure the effectiveness of it. Also, the instructor must know and take their students' interest, background and experience into account in order to present a problem or situation that will motivate the student to reflect, research and learn to acquire new knowledge.

3C3R PBL Problem Designing Model

According to Hung, Jonassen and Liu (2008), a number of researchers (Lee, 1999; Duch, 2001; Weiss, 2003; Hung, 2006a) have discussed and provided suggestions and guidelines for designing PBL problems. For instance, Lee (1999) proposed a decision model for problem selection in which selection of the PBL problem is a function of learning objectives, prior knowledge, domain knowledge, problem structured and complexity, and time availability. Also, Duch (2001) suggested a process of five stages of writing PBL problems (choose a central idea, think of a real-world context for the concept, stage the problem to lead students' research, write a teacher's guide, and identify resources for students). Aiming at promoting higher order thinking, Weiss (2003) suggested several principles for designing PBL problems, including considering students' prior knowledge, using ill-structured and authentic problems, and promoting collaborative, lifelong, and self-directed learning.

However, these design guidelines, principles, and processes were inadequate for providing educators and practitioners with a complete conceptual framework and the systematic design process required for designing effective PBL problems for learners across disciplines and ages (Hung et al., 2008). Therefore, to provide PBL educators and practitioners with a systematic conceptual framework for designing effective and reliable PBL problems, Hung (2006a) introduced the 3C3R model as a conceptual framework for systematically designing optimal PBL problems. The 3C3R PBL problem design model is a systematic method specifically designed to guide instructional designers and educators to design effective PBL problems for all levels and across disciplines of learners. Figure 2 is a diagram of this model.

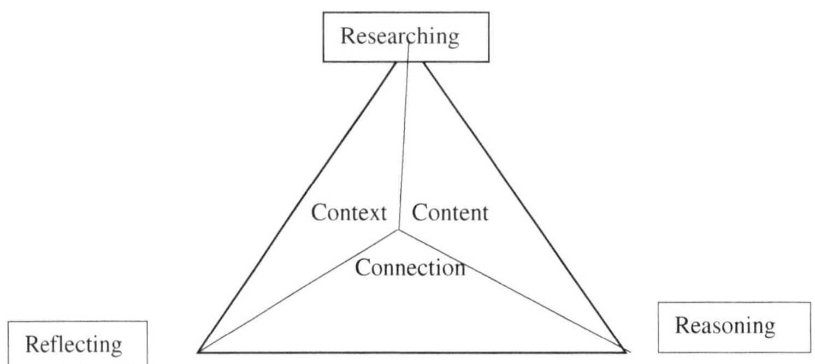

Figure 1: 3R3C Problem Designing Model
Source: Hung (2006a)

The 3C3R model has two classes of components namely, core components and processing components. The core components include content, context, and connection. Furthermore, the core components are primarily concerned with the issues of appropriateness and sufficiency of content knowledge, knowledge contextualization, and knowledge integration. On the other hand, the processing components include researching, reasoning, and reflecting, which deal with students' acquisition of content knowledge and the development of problem-solving skills and self-directed learning skills.

From the 3C3R PBL problem designing model, it seems the instructor using PBL method should determine the content knowledge and the context in which the knowledge should be explored as well as how they can draw on ideas or knowledge to solve the problem. In addition, the instructor or the facilitator should be guided by the fact that the problem presented for the learners to inquire into will trigger students to critically reason, research and reflect on the problem or the topic given. This will determine the kind of knowledge the student will acquire, skills they will develop and how it influences students' self-directed learning skills. Hence, a geography tutor employing problem-based learning as a method of instruction in geography must ensure that the content, context and connection analysis of the problem or topic are done. This is important because there are a lot of things in our environment that can attract the attention of the learners, hence, outlining the context in which the problem should be dealt with will help learners to be focused and integrate their previous knowledge with other experiences to solve the problem. Also, the problem or issues presented to students to inquire into should challenge students to reason critically, research and reflect in order to acquire the right knowledge, develop their problem solving and self-directed learning skills.

Problem-Based Learning Implementation Process in Geography Education

The implementation of problem-based learning instruction in geographic education frequently incorporates Geographic Information Systems technologies (Quain, 2014). In geography classrooms, GIS is an effective tool to use with PBL instruction (Bednarz, 2004). This is due to the fact that GIS is interactive and it helps students learn how to read maps (Shin, 2006). Following the creation of the 3C3R model, Hung (2006b) further developed a nine-step problem design process to operationalize the conceptual framework into a step-by-step process:

Step 1. Set goals and objectives.
Step 2. Conduct content/task analysis.
Step 3. Analyze context specification.
Step 4. Select/generate PBL problem.
Step 5. Conduct PBL problem affordance analysis.
Step 6. Conduct correspondence analysis.
Step 7. Conduct calibration processes.
Step 8. Construct reflection component.
Step 9. Examine inter-supporting relationships of 3C3R components

Also, Hung et al. (2008) outlined four steps in PBL designing process

1. Students in groups of five to eight encounter and reason through the problem. They attempt to define and bound the problem, set learning goals by identifying what they know already, what hypotheses or conjectures they can think of, what they need to learn to better understand the dimensions of the problem, what learning activities are required and who would perform them.

2. During self-directed study, individual students complete their learning assignments. They collect and study resources and prepare reports to the group.

3. Students share their learning with the group and revisit the problem, generating additional hypotheses and rejecting others based on their learning.

4. At the end of the learning period (usually one week), students summarize and integrate their learning.

According to Dahlgren (2003), problem-based learning (PBL) begins when students are confronted with an open-ended, ill-structured, authentic (real-world) problem and work in teams to identify learning needs and develop a viable solution, with instructors acting as facilitators rather than primary sources of information. Here, Duch (2001) indicates that class time may be devoted to:

i. Groups reporting out their progress on previous learning issues and listing their current learning issues and plans of work,

ii. Minilectures giving information on issues being dealt with by all groups, clarifying common difficulties, and suggesting additional learning issues, and

iii. Whole class discussion.

Furthermore, Padmavathy and Mareesh (2013) outline seven steps of problem-based learning. They include:

1. Explain unknown wording, statements and concepts;
2. Define the problem(s);
3. Brainstorm – analyse/try to explain the problem(s);
4. Formulate learning issues and define action to be taken;
5. Self-Directed Learning;
6. Subsequent Group Meetings: Report and evaluate on self-directed learning. Refine learning issues and define further action; and
7. Report Phase: Resolution of problem. Evaluation of process.

The prior submissions imply that a well-designed problem should first define the objectives of the problem process, specify the content and the context in which students should work to solve the problem before students go out to explore or find solutions to the problem. This step is necessary for students to appreciate and comprehend the problem concept very well and know what they are expected to do as they work on the problem. This may minimise or prevent the confusion or uncertainty that may arise from students' groups concerning the problem studied. In addition, grouping of students in the PBL process should fall between five to eight in order to ensure effective task accomplishment. This is because forming large groups of students (ten and above) may result in a situation where some students would not participate in the task given.

Further, regular reports should be given by the student to collectively ascertain the progress of the problem resolution. This may enable students and the facilitator to offer constructive criticism and guidance to arrive at the problem solution. So Weiss (2003) notes that a well-designed problem guides students to use course content and methods, illustrates fundamental principles, concepts, and procedures, and perhaps induces the students to infer those things for themselves instead of getting them directly from the instructor.

Also, it engages the students in the types of reflection and activities that lead to higher-order learning. Problems may vary significantly in scope, from single-topic and single-discipline problems that can be solved in a matter of days to multidisciplinary problems that may take an entire semester to solve (Weiss, 2003; Tan, 2003). Hence, for PBL to be used effectively in geography education, the lecturer (facilitator) must be well-equipped with these steps and skills of the problem designing process in order to guide his/her students with the right information to get right feedback form the problem task and vice versa. This is because Schmidt, Rotgans and Yew (2011) and Hung (2011) on their elaboration of cognitive constructivist process of PBL indicate that the facilitator provide scaffold, a framework on which students can construct knowledge relating to the problem. It is this scaffold provided which helps student groups to develop possible theories or hypotheses to explain the problem and also identify learning issues to be researched.

Challenges affecting the effective Implementation of PBL in Geography Education

Problem-based learning is a new instructional strategy in the discipline of Geography (Pawson et al., 2006; Spronken-Smith, 2005). In addition, the National Geography Standards (include a focus on "Doing Geography" which emphasizes the problem-based learning philosophy (Heffron & Downs, 2012). However, studies (Chakravathi & Heleagrahara, 2010; Egidius, 1999; Mansor et al., 2015; Luk, 2004; Wee, 2000; Omoro & Nato, 2014; Pagander & Read; 2014) have shown that teachers experience difficulties implementing such instructional approaches in their classrooms. Some of the challenges include large classroom size, educational system and curriculum structure; resources (time, money and logistics), traditional/convectional assumptions of the students, student assessment and the suitability of the PBL for all students, both strong and weaker students.

Large classroom size and group work challenge

According to Egidius (1999), one of the major problems a teacher faces using the PBL method is large classroom sizes. He explained that due to the number of students in a class, there are very few classes in which one can conduct a PBL session. Egidius suggests that the optimal group size should be between five to eight students (p. 52). To be able to conduct a PBL session the teacher needs to divide the class into several small groups and guide all of them at the same time, resulting in difficulties for the teacher in following each group's progress and problems. In supporting Egidius, Nasr and Ramadan (2008) pointed that students found it challenging to find time to meet with their group members outside of class. In addition, some students were resistant to group work and student centred work (Keller, 2002).

Also, Bonwell (1998) revealed that class sizes are too big to permit the use of PBL. Further, Luk (2004) found that instructors/teachers have difficulty in maintaining and guaranteeing the effectiveness of learning with a large number of groups in a class. Traylor (as cited in Otabil, Dufie, Tandoh & Damoah-Mensah, 2014) notes that, a well-equipped class with space and the least amount of distractions will usually help teachers to have more interactive and practical instructional lesson. In addition, it also helps students, especially with learning difficulties to focus on instructions of the teacher.

These submissions show that using PBL as a method of teaching geography warrants a well-equipped classroom, spacious and standard class size (5-8). This is because large class size makes supervision and evaluation difficult since there is a number of groups to be supervised and evaluated. This negatively affects the effective use of the method as is alluded to by Egidius.

Educational system and curriculum structure Challenge

Further, Bonwell (1998) pointed out that due to the imposed accountability, the structure of curriculum and educational system makes it difficult for PBL instruction to be used effectively. He further indicated that teachers believe Problem-based or discovery learning will not cover the course content and will require too much preparation and learning time. Many geography teachers or instructors see the geography curriculum to be too overloaded to be completed within the given time or years. Hence, teachers preparing students for exams stick to methods that will easily make them finish the syllabus within the given time. Also, Wee (2000) revealed that the traditional assessment system did not aid in the implementation of PBL. Thus, the benefits of PBL were undermined because students were more interested in studying for their examinations and ensuring that they graduated with flying colours. According to Vogler and Virtue (2007) "teachers under the pressure of high stakes [testing] tend to use teacher-centred instructional practices, such as lecture, instead of student-centred approaches" (p. 56). That may be explained by schools' accountability to standardized testing (Mitchell, 2009).

These submissions infer that PBL method cannot be assessed effectively through the traditional assessment system (Paper and Pen/pencil exams or test). Hence, adopting PBL as a method of teaching geography, means the geography curriculum must be restructured based on PBL philosophy or ideas. These includes enough time allocation for the geography, workshops and seminars for students as well as assessment system focusing on student creativity, problem-solving, teamwork among others.

Resource Challenge (time, money and logistics)

Another factor which studies (Farrant, 1996; Omoro & Nato, 2014; Pagander & Read, 2014) have shown as affecting the effective use of PBL method is the resources involved. For instance, Pagander and Read pointed out that the transformation from the traditional teaching methods to a PBL-centred teaching method takes time and money. Although students generally like, and gain greater ability to solve real-life problems in, problem-based learning courses, instructors using this methodology must often invest more time to assess student learning and prepare course materials, as compared to the Lecture method (Vernom, 1995).

In addition, the time needed for teacher supervision and advice to individuals or groups in PBL is much greater than that required in conventional teaching (Luk, 2004). Also, Luk revealed that teachers found PBL to be time-consuming, which meant that they had to sacrifice their own free time to cater for students' needs. Furthermore, Tamakloe, Amedahe and Atta (1996) indicate that time constraint is another element facing the teaching of geography in schools. In addition, the time taken for the study trip is considered by some teachers to be excessive in terms of the rewards it would yield (Omoro & Nato, 2014).

Besides, Sarkar and Frazier (as cited in Otabil et al., 2014) found a longer list of reasons why fieldwork was not being used as a method of teaching from a broader perspective. These include insufficient time, inability to manage diverse groups outside of the classroom, schools not allowing field trips, scheduling difficulties, and a renewed test focus because of the "No Child Left Behind" policy in the USA. This emphasized the warning by Grimwade (2000) that unless more teaching time is allocated to geography, there is the danger that geography's subject integrity will be compromised and that this could affect the long term visibility of the subject. According to Nasr and Ramadan (2008), evaluation of PBL in a thermodynamics course highlighted that the instructor needed to plan for more interaction time with students during class and allow students a significant amount of in-class time to work in their groups. Likewise, Keller (2002) noted that students needed additional time in class because they struggled to find time outside of class for group work, a common element of PBL. In addition, due to lack of instructional tools and models for PBL in ATE programs, those seeking to use and extend the use of this pedagogical method have to dedicate a great deal of time to developing innovative curriculum and training educators (Craft & Mack, 2001; Keller, 2002; Massa, Dischino, Donnelly, Hanes & DeLaura, 2012).

Besides, Omoro and Nato (2014) are of the view that there are high costs involved when the students are to travel to distant places, and the travelling risks that the students are exposed to, make PBL a very rare method to be used by teachers in teaching geography. Also, Farrant (1996) said that the financial commitment to the method (PBL) is very high, especially if the phenomenon is distant from the school. He further indicates that inadequate logistics, such as school bus and cameras, make it difficult to embark on fieldwork which is a PBL learning. This is due to the fact that some of the problems the teacher may give to students to explore or discover demands that they travel outside their school campus. Hence, the absence of logistics, bus, and financial commitment hinder the use of PBL as a method of instruction in geography. According to Berkson (as cited in Burch, Yeld, Seggie & Schmidt, 2007), the findings of a study conducted in South Africa, focusing on the implementation and the effectiveness of PBL, says that PBL has "considerable potential implications for medical education in South Africa in the face of the relatively greater financial costs inherent in PBL programs" (p. 355). This implies that for PBL method to be used as a method of instruction in geography, enough time should be allocated, financial commitment and logistics must be made available. This is so because PBL demands more time, energy and travels, which when used would not be replaced by the school; and also the students have a given time frame or years to be taught to write their final exams.

Traditional/convectional assumptions of the students

According to Reithlingshoefer (1992), one of the challenges affecting the effective use of problem-based learning is the traditional assumptions of the students. He explained that most of the students might have spent their previous years of education assuming their teacher as the main disseminator of knowledge. Therefore, due to this understanding about the subject matter, students may lack the ability to simply wonder about something in the initial years of problem-based learning. This is supported by the findings of Wee (2000) which indicated that students at Temasek Polytechnic found the PBL curriculum confusing, uncertain and ambiguous. This is because under conventional teaching methods, students look up to their teacher as content provider and endorser of knowledge. With PBL, students are required to identify problem statements and proceed to answer them. Furthermore, Chakravathi and Heleagrahara (2010) found that years of the conventional learning mode have negative effects on students' learning process. Thus students are not prepared to be empowered by taking responsibility for their own learning, which involves searching for information independently and collaboratively. Additionally, trust between group members is usually not firmly established. Besides, several students also asked for more traditional teaching and learning, such as material that they could take notes on and tests (Keller, 2002).

Student assessment Challenge

One of the major problems a teacher working with PBL faces is with the manner of assessing the students' work and progress (Pagander & Read, 2014). To accomplish this, teachers need to use methods other than simply providing the student with an exam which will test their rote knowledge of a subject, or giving them a grade on a paper written. A PBL assignment is based on problem-solving skills through group work. The question to be answered here is: how do you assess a student's problem solving skills? Further, how do you test, or assess, interaction or group work? Tai and Yuen (2007) states that when "assessing PBL, authentic assessment seems as a more appropriate means to assess learning compared to traditional assessments such as norm-reference and standardized testing that assesses recall of factual content knowledge" (p. 2).

MacDonald (2005) described that "the assessment phase should focus on evaluating acts of creativity, problem-solving, self-management, and teamwork" (p. 5). However, it takes much more effort and practice from the teachers to be able to apply the different methods of assessment in a correct and functional way. Ellis and Hafner (2008) indicated that an assessment of the assignment is difficult and time consuming" (p. 180). Besides, Nasr and Ramadan (2008) reported challenges with carrying out proper assessment while also assuring appropriate skill acquisition. Another issue is self-assessment in PBL. The students participating in a PBL session "have to make statements about what they already know and can do and where there are gaps in their knowledge and competences" (Macdonald, 2005, p. 86). Teaching the students how to self-assess will be an important part of the teacher's job and seems to be a burden to the instructor. This is because the teacher/instructor has to take a lot of time in planning how to manifest such assessment technique in PBL. Hence, most instructors prefer the traditional teaching and assessment system which is stressful and time consuming as pointed out by Bonwell (1998).

Development of PBL process skills factor

Mansor et al. (2015) revealed that the most critical problems encountered in using PBL is the development of PBL process skills. These include skills such as thinking skills and information searching skills. According to Mansor et al., "students are quite weak in using thinking skills; that's the greatest problem actually, not so much on analytical skills, but thinking skills itself, the students are lacking-how to think out of the box." (p. 263). In addition, the students are also not resourceful in searching for information. Furthermore, they don't even know how to ask for help, who to reach out for. Some even resort to the cut and paste culture, which is quite rampant and made easy by technology." However, in PBL, student have to search for information independently, decide what to look for and reasoning thorough about the problem in order to solve the problem given to students. This situation affects the effectiveness of PBL as an instructional approach since student are frail in using thinking and information searching skills.

In a nutshell, it is clearly established from the above submissions that large classroom size, educational system and curriculum structure, resources (time, money and logistics), traditional/convectional assumptions of the students, student assessment and the suitability of the PBL for both stronger and weaker students are some of the critical factors that affect the effective implementation of PBL instruction at various levels of the educational ladder. Therefore, a critical look at this situation should be done to ensure that the environment, which is the true laboratory for geography students and teachers, is regularly visited and used for their search or experiment to achieve maximum output or performance of the students. This is why the researcher sought to find out whether such challenges exist among University of Cape Coast geography students.

Effective Ways of Implementing Problem-Based Learning in Geography Education

Mansor et al. (2015) suggested a number of ways to make implementation of PBL effective. First, on the issue of development of process skills, students need to be taught and trained on how to be more independent in their search for knowledge rather than to just wait for the teacher to tell them what they should learn. In addition, they should be taught thinking tools such as mind mapping, and make them aware of the rich resources of information, which are not limited to the Internet. Furthermore, students should be encouraged to use the library and train them on how to cite articles from journals as well as the importance of primary sources of information, with the internet serving as a supporting informational source, rather than simply copying and pasting (Mansor et al., 2015, pp. 263-264). Besides, curriculum-related issues such as coverage have to be evaluated continuously. As such, constant review of the curriculum and consistent monitoring of PBL classroom practices must be made a priority and must also be the norm to ensure that the educational goals of producing enterprising, employable, versatile and knowledgeable graduates are achieved. Further, Poikela and Poikela (2005) established that to be able to use PBL as a teaching method, the curriculum must provide goals and guidelines according to this method. This means that a curriculum based on the ideas of PBL needs to be used by the school, with the result that the entire school works with the PBL method, and not separate classes (p. 58). This corresponds with Egidius' (1999) idea that one can use

PBL as a complement to other teaching methods. To be able to do this, the teacher must make sure that what he has planned as a PBL activity follows the goals and guidelines of the school curriculum, which will provide a lot of extra time and work for the teacher. Additionally, Tiangco (as cited in Tai & Yuen, 2007) writes that "the assessment phase should focus on evaluating acts of creativity, problem-solving, self-management, and teamwork" (p. 5). However, it takes much more effort and practice from the teachers to be able to apply the different methods of assessment in a correct and functional way. According to Amu, Kwao, Mensah and Tengfah (2012), time allocations for the teaching of geography should be increased to effectively employ problem-based learning method to the fullness.

Rogers (2014) pointed out that the adoption and continued use of PBL requires support and guidance for students and the instructor. In addition, Rogers revealed that supports and guidance are needed from administration, instructor as guide and professional development. For example, a majority of participants in his study discussed how support from administration affected their ability to successfully implement PBL. "All participants expressed that they must guide their students through the transition into PBL because it differs from their experiences with more traditional teaching and learning. Additionally, all participants looked upon their PBL specific professional development quite favourably and recommended it for those ATE community college instructors looking to implement the teaching method" (Rogers. 2014, pp. 60-61). Again, Rogers reported that PBL specific professional development that they experienced was beneficial. He further indicated that "participants gained others' perspectives, gained tools to help with implementation challenges and learned how to develop their own curriculum through PBL specific professional development work" (p. 69). Therefore, participants advised instructors wanting to teach through PBL to engage in professional development training and to use pre-developed curriculum. Based on these findings, Rogers recommended the following to help facilitators to overcome the factors that hinder effective implementation of the PBL method;

According to Rogers (2014), to be an effective facilitator of PBL and help overcome the implementation challenge of student reluctance, instructors will need to initially guide students through the PBL process and must exercise patience with students as they adjust to a different learning style.

1. In addition, facilitators should scaffold the difficulty of problems presented and resist giving students answers. Serving as a guide, instructors must provide more support to students initially, while giving them more and more autonomy to direct their own learning as they become comfortable with the teaching method.

2. To accomplish these goals, PBL practitioners should design curricula that teaches students a formula for problem solving and provides students with tools to practice this formula.

3. Again, Rogers opined that the ability to analyse and solve problems on their own will give students the confidence with the pedagogical practice and the ability to work autonomously and in teams, without direct supervision from their instructor. Once students are comfortable with a uniform and expected problem solving process, instructors can begin giving students more difficult problems and provide students more autonomy.

4. Additionally, instructors need to be explicit with students through clear guidelines and provide a thorough explanation of what will be expected of them, before PBL implementation begins.

Besides, Briggs (2015) explains ten (10) strategies adapted from Stanford University Newsletter on Teaching, as effective ways of using PBL instructional approach. The strategies include:

1. Clearly define your purpose for doing PBL: Know the procedures you will use, along with your expectations, well before your first PBL session.

2. Hold brainstorming sessions: The first few class meetings in a PBL course include brainstorming sessions in which issues central to the course are identified.

3. Develop ill-structured problems: Based on student input about course topics, the instructor develops ill-structured problems, or open-ended problems that have multiple solutions and require students "to look at many methods before deciding on a particular solution". Ill-structured problems require more information for understanding the problem than is initially available; contain multiple solution paths; change as new information is obtained; prevent students from knowing that they have made the "right" decision; generate interest and controversy and cause the learner to ask questions; are open-ended and complex enough to require collaboration and thinking beyond recall; and contain content that is authentic to the discipline.

4. Refrain from providing information: Regardless of how topics were selected, the instructor presents the problems to student groups before providing any formal instruction on the topic. Allen, Duch and Groh (1996) however, suggest that problems be introduced with "mini-lectures" that provide some context for the problem and identify areas of potential difficulty.

5. Allow time for collaboration: Students then work on the problems in groups of three to eight students, depending on the number of students in the course and the number of available instructors or tutors. Both inside and outside of school time, students work with their groups to solve problems. Throughout each

session the instructor must ensure that all students are involved in the problem-solving process and must familiarize students with the resources needed (e.g. library references, databases) to solve the problems, as well as identify common difficulties or misconceptions.

6. Emphasize depth over breadth: Give students two to six weeks to work on one problem depending on its complexity. Upon completing the research or inquiry phase of problem solving, groups may be required to write a report and present it to the rest of the class.

7. Conduct regular assessment: Assess progress at regular intervals. If necessary, interrupt group work to correct misconceptions, or to bring groups up to par with one another.

8. Hold class discussions: Allow time for class discussion of the problem at the end of the PBL session, or at the beginning of the next class period.

9. Facilitate peer feedback: A critical part of assessment in PBL is the feedback students receive from their peers. Allen, Duch, and Groh (1996) asked students to rate their group members using a numerical scale based on "attendance, degree of preparation for class, listening and communication skills, ability to bring new and relevant information to the group, and ability to support and improve the functioning of the group as a whole". This peer rating constituted up to ten percent of students' final grades.

10. Assess authentically: PBL assessments should be authentic, which is to say that they should be structured so that students can display their understanding of problems and their solutions in contextually-meaningful ways (Gallagher, 1997). Clearly, multiple-choice assessments and even short-answer or essay questions that require rote repetition of facts will be of little value in assessing the extent to which students have internalized holistic approaches to complex problems.

Besides, Genareo and Lyons (2015) describes six (6) ways PBL can be effectively implemented. These include identifying outcomes/Assessment, designing the scenario, introducing PBL, research, product performance and assessment.

i. Identify Outcomes/Assessment: PBL fits best with process-oriented course outcomes such as collaboration, research, and problem solving. It can help students acquire content or conceptual knowledge, or develop disciplinary habits such as writing or communication. After determining whether your course has learning outcomes that fit with PBL, you will develop formative and summative assessments to measure student learning. Group contracts, self/peer-evaluation forms, learning reflections, writing samples, and rubrics are potential PBL assessments.

ii. Design the Scenario: Next, you design the PBL scenario with an embedded problem that will emerge through student brainstorming. Think of a real, complex issue related to your course content. It's seldom difficult to identify lots of problems in our fields; the key is writing a scenario for our students that will elicit the types of thinking, discussion, research, and learning that need to take place to meet the learning outcomes. Scenarios should be motivating, interesting, and generate good discussion.

iii. Introduce PBL: If PBL is new to your students, you can practice with an "easy problem," such as a scenario about long lines in the dining hall. After grouping students and allowing time to engage in an abbreviated version of PBL, introduce the assignment expectations, rubrics, and timelines. Then let groups read through the scenario(s). You might develop a single scenario and let each group tackle it in their own way, or you could design multiple scenarios addressing a unique problem for each group to discuss and research on.

iv. Research: PBL research begins with small-group brainstorming sessions where students define the problem and determine what they know about the problem (background knowledge), what they need to learn more about (topics to research), and where they need to look to find data (databases, interviews, etc.). Groups should write the problem as a statement or research question. They will likely need assistance. Think about your own research: without good research questions, the process can be unguided or far too specific. Students should decide upon group roles and assign responsibility for researching topics necessary for them to fully understand their problems. Students then develop an initial hypothesis to "test" as they research a solution. Remember: research questions and hypotheses can change after students find information disconfirming their initial beliefs.

v. Product performance: After researching, the students create products and presentations that synthesize their research, solutions, and learning. The format of the summative assessment is completely up to you. We treat this step like a research fair. Students find resources to develop background knowledge that informs their understanding, and then they collaboratively present their findings, including one or more viable solutions, as research posters to the class.

vi. Assessment: During the PBL assessment step, evaluate the groups' products and performances. Use rubrics to determine whether students have clearly communicated the problem, background, research methods, solutions (feasible and research-based), and resources, and to decide whether all group members participated meaningfully. You should consider having your students fill out reflections about their learning (including what they've learned about the content and the research process) every day, and at the conclusion of the process.

From the above submission, restricting the geography curriculum and the assessment system to suit the PBL method may help ensure its effective implementation. In addition, support and guidance form administration in terms resources (time, money and logistics) and encouraging specific PBL professional training and development for instructors who are facilitators may result in the effective implementation of Problem-based learning method in geography in education. Besides, the ways or stages outlined by some researchers (Briggs, 2015; Genareo & Lyons, 2015 among others) when critically followed may help implement PBL method in geography education effectively.

Benefits of Effective Implementation of Problem-Based Learning (PBL) in Geography Education

PBL approach to learning according to Savin-Baden (2001) is characterized by flexibility and diversity in the sense that it can be implemented in a variety of ways in different subjects and disciplines in diverse contexts. Several researchers (Baker & White, 2003; Brickell & Herrington, 2006; Quain, 2014; Havorson & Wescoat, 2002; Patterson et al., 2003; Tulloch & Graff, 2007) have revealed that problem-based learning is an efficacious instructional method or strategy for improving students' knowledge in various levels of geography. Some of the benefits or importance of adopting PBL as an instructional method include:

Develops student intellectual/ analytical and problem solving skills

PBL is argued as a learning method that can promote the development of critical thinking skills (Şendağ & Ferhan-Odabasi, 2009). Thus, in PBL learning, students learn how to analyze a problem, identify relevant facts and generate hypotheses, identify necessary information/ knowledge for solving the problem and make reasonable judgments about solving the problem. That is why Hung et al. (2008) pointed that one of the essential promises of PBL is improving students' problem-solving skills. Since PBL starts with a problem to be solved, it allows students to actively solve realistic problems similar to those faced by people outside the classroom every day (Mergendoller, Maxwell & Bellisimo, 2006; Béneker, Sanders, Tani, Taylor & van der Vaart, 2007). Since PBL is based on real-life situations, students gain self confidence in their ability to resolve problems that they might face in everyday activities. Therefore, being able to successfully solve problems in the classroom can correlate to self confidence in solving problems outside the classroom as is pointed out by Mergendoller et al. Also, PBL helps students develop deeper analytical skills (Utecht, 2003). He indicated that analytical skills such as critical thinking, problem defining and problem solving are at the heart of PBL. Students use these skills by considering possible solutions to a problem. Additionally, students start to develop skills such as research techniques, data analysis and working as a team member as they move through these analytical skills.

Moreso, as students become more accustomed to the PBL learning environment they start to mature intellectually. Moreover, Kuruganti, Needham and Zundel (2012) revealed in their study that the problem-solving skills acquired in the first attempt at solving a problem are carried on to, and improves, the next attempt. Though the study does not imply that PBL improves knowledge retention, it does suggest that the problem-solving skill is developed through repeated use of the method. Besides, Gentry (2000, p. 13) identifies "self-confidence, desire to achieve, analytical skills and teamwork abilities, as intellectual skills students learn that might not be prevalent in a traditional classroom format". All of these skills assist students in becoming lifelong learners. Gallagher et al. (1992) in an experiment found that PBL students showed a significant increase in the use of the problem-finding step from pretest to post-test, which was a critical problem-solving technique. In contrast, in the post-test, the comparison group tended to skip the problem-finding step and move directly from the fact-finding step to the implementation step. The result suggested that PBL is effective in fostering students' development of appropriate problem-solving processes and skills. Moreover, PBL has shown a positive impact on students' abilities to apply basic science knowledge and transfer problem-solving skills in real-world professional or personal situations. Lohman and Finkelstein (1999) found that the first-year dental education students in a 10-month PBL program improved significantly in their near transfer of problem-solving skills by an average of 31.3%, and their far transfer of problem-solving skills increased by an average of 23.1%. Based on their data, they suggested that repeated exposure to PBL was the key to facilitating the development of problem-solving skills. Several studies have shown that PBL has very positive effects on students' transfer of problem-solving skills to workplaces.

Woods (1996) reported that employers praised McMaster University's PBL chemical engineering graduates' outstanding problem-solving skills and job performance. Further, Scholkmann and Roters (2009) conducted a study on "the effects of PBL and the professional development of teachers in Germany, Sweden, and the Netherlands. This study concluded that there were no negative effects on the acquisition of knowledge but positive effects on self-assessment abilities, better performance in problem solving and in practical tests" (p. 5). They cite positive mood alongside problem-based testing, formative evaluation, and portfolios as keys to success (Scholkmann & Roters, 2009). The above submissions imply that adopting PBL as an instructional method in geography education will enlighten and develop geography students' observational, intellectual, analytical and problem solving skills. These are very essential in geography education since observation and analytical skills are critical tools for geographic study. Further, geography deals with the patterns of process and phenomena that affect human and environment relationship and so as students through PBL explore these features, it helps solve the problems in our environment.

Promotes student-centred/self-directed learning/life-long learning

The proponents of PBL argued that it promotes authentic learning and that it engenders metacognitive awareness (Major & Palmer, 2001; Benson, 2003). PBL is self-directed and as students start to realize the connections between their academics and the world around them, they can start to answer the often heard question, "When will I ever use this?" PBL helps to show students that there is a direct correlation between school and real-world problems, thus the desire to achieve is heightened by this knowledge that "I can use this in the real-world" (Utecht, 2003). He further indicates that PBL does not just allow students to be an active participant in the learning process, but forces them to take an active role by engaging them in a meaningful, thought provoking way.

Besides, Schmidt, Rotgans and Yew (2011) pointed out that PBL addresses the need to promote lifelong learning through the process of inquiry and constructivist learning. In addition, Schmidt, Loyens, Van-Gog and Paas (2007) indicate that PBL can be considered a constructivist approach to instruction, emphasizing collaborative and self-directed learning and being supported by flexible teacher scaffolding. Conferring to Antepohl and Herzig (1999), students are actively involved in Problem-based learning and they like this method. In agreement to Antepohl et al., Vernon and Blake (1993) indicate that students themselves resolve the problems that are given to them, they take more interest and responsibility for their learning. In addition, they themselves look for resources like research articles, journals, web materials etc. for their purpose. This equips them with more proficiency in seeking resources in comparison to the students of traditional learning methods. Also, it fosters active learning, retention and development of lifelong learning skills as found by Spencer and Jordan (1999) that PBL encourages self-directed learning by confronting students with problems and stimulates the development of deep learning.

Therefore, PBL aids in giving students tools to become lifelong learners, tools that cannot be taught out of a text book, but only by being an integral part of the learning. Further, Hung, Jonassen and Liu (2008) reveal that through actively executing problem-solving processes and observing tutors modeling problem-solving, reasoning, and metacognitive processes, PBL students learn how to think and learn independently. This is why Hung et al., opined that the ultimate goal of PBL is to educate students to be self-directed, independent, life-long learners. This confirms Pawson et al. (2006) who identified positive benefits for students, academic and institutions and noted that students developed lifelong skills and found PBL a more enjoyable experience. This in turn leads to improving job satisfaction for academics. Where there is support for using PBL for academic reasons, it appears to be qualified with most authors reporting only a moderate improvement when compared to more traditional methods (Sanson-Fisher & Lynagh, 2005; Colliver, 2000). PBL has also been shown to promote self-directed learning and the adoption of a deep (meaning-oriented) approach to learning, as opposed to a superficial (memorization-based) approach (Blumberg, 2000; Felder & Brent, 2005).

From the submissions above, it denotes that employing a problem-based learning technique in teaching and learning geography develops students' observational and team work skills which are necessary in the studies of geography as a subject. This is because observation is one of the tool of the geographer. In addition, it promotes self-directed learning, understanding of concepts, facts, principles, theories and generalizations in geography. These, in the long term, improve academic achievement of geography students.

Reinforces students' communication, interpersonal and teamwork skills

Project-based learning involves more teamwork and collaborative learning. The teams or groups resolve relevant problems in collaboration, hence it fosters student interaction, teamwork and reinforces interpersonal skills like peer evaluation, working with group dynamics etc. (Vernon, 1995). It also nurses the leadership qualities in them, teaches them to make decision by consensus and give constructive feedback to team members etc. (Tricia & Moore, 2007). Furthermore, by working in a team, students learn to be responsible to other learners. They learn to set both long and short term goals as they relate to the problem. Students learn to communicate effectively with other members of a team and learn the importance of effective communication. These skills are what, according to the business world, students lack when entering the workplace; facilitating exchange of opinions and insight, creating positive social interactions, exerting a combination of diverse strengths and backgrounds in teams, sharing workload, fostering debate and compromise, building trust relationship between group members and enhancing leadership skills (Keeling, 2008), the importance of self-control of the study schedule (Cheong, 2008), having flexibility which enables them to complete tasks (time, presentation, focus and pace) and sharing opinions and perspectives (Pepper, 2009).

Studies (Schmidt & van der Molen, 2001; Schmidt et al., 2006) revealed that PBL graduates rated themselves better prepared professionally than their counterparts in terms of interpersonal skills, cooperation skills, problem-solving skills, self-directed learning, information gathering, professional skills and the ability to work and plan efficiently and independently. According to Mansur, Kayastha, Makaju and Dongol (2012), students do independent, self-directed study before returning to the group to discuss and refine their acquired knowledge. Thus, PBL is not about problem solving per se, but rather it uses appropriate problems to increase knowledge and understanding. Additionally, Mansur et al., indicated that group learning facilitates not only the acquisition of knowledge but also several other desirable attributes, such as communication skills, teamwork, problem solving, independent responsibility for learning, sharing information, and respect for others.

Moreso, Vardi and Ciccarelli (2008) revealed that employers have appreciated the positive attributes of communication, teamwork, respect and collaboration that PBL students have developed. These skills provide for better future skills preparation in the ever-changing information explosion. Furthermore, studies (Chung & Chow, 2004; Gijbel, Dochy, Van den Bossche & Seger, 2005; Pepper, 2009; Lim & Lew, 2012) have found a vigorous positive effect of PBL on skill development, understanding the interconnections between concepts, deep conceptual understanding, ability to apply appropriate metacognitive and reasoning strategies, teamwork skills, and even class attendance, but have not reached any firm conclusion about the effect on content knowledge. Pepper (2009) conducted a study on Problem-based learning in science at the University of Western Australia, and his findings described students as being happy to work in groups though less comfortable about delivering oral presentations for group assessment. In addition, the students enjoyed listening to and sharing different perspectives, which implies that they were working collaboratively and constructing new knowledge. Conferring to Allen et al, (n.d.) the power of working collaboratively fosters strong communication and interpersonal skills while harnessing the power of different thinking and learning styles. Many students however, were less enamoured with presenting their solutions orally to an audience. Besides, Lim and Lew's (2012) study on the topic "Does academic performance affect the challenges faced by students in their initial adaptation to a problem-based learning environment?" follows 1019 students in their first year at an unnamed local polytechnic school which uses PBL as its sole method in diploma programs. The first result demonstrated that previous academic performance had no significant effect on the challenges faced by students and that PBL was not detrimental to weaker students but did show that weaker students outperformed stronger students in problem-solving skills (p. 7).

In addition, the second result demonstrated a strong correlation between teamwork and performance, supporting the claim that good, positive interaction with others in the team leads to better performance, which is one of the core concepts of PBL pedagogy (Lim & Lew, 2012). Hence, PBL in geography education may be efficacious in developing geography students' communicative, interpersonal skills and team work abilities since they work in groups or teams. Additionally, PBL taught as a small group teaching method in geography may aid the combination of the acquisition of geographic knowledge with the development of generic skills and attitudes in geography as a discipline.

Promotes students' self-perception, confidence and self-motivated attitude

Bruner (1966) points out that every individual has the will to learn and this will must be used in activities which would raise curiosity and direct students to studying and discovering knowledge. He further states that learning happens by discovery, which prioritizes reflection, thinking, experimenting, and exploring. People who use self-discovery in learning turn out to be more self-confident. According to Hung et al. (2008), students have positive perception on the effects of PBL. Further, Harlen (as cited in Balım, 2009) states that "inquiry learning in science develops students' perception skills. This is because it allows them to understand the natural phenomena and the world by using their cognitive and physical skills" (p. 2). It is suggested that this kind of learning shows students the nature of scientific studies and the ways in which learning is realized. Thus, it develops their discovery skills (National Research Council [NRC], 2004). Therefore, PBL requires active participation of students in the learning process (Matson, 2006). Also, Havorson and Wescoat (2002) and Spronken-Smith (2005) studied problem-based learning in geography at the college undergraduate level and the results included increasing positive attitudes towards geography through problem-based learning instruction. Additionally, Drennon (2005); Tulloch and Graff (2007) also tested students' geographic attitudes using problem-based learning instructional approach and found that students' attitudes towards geography education improved through the use of these PBL strategies.

Moreover, Klein (1995) showed that problem-based learning also helps to increase students' attitudes and motivations in other ways. For example, Klein (1995) states that in order to "build feelings of empowerment in students, classroom activities should give students an idea of what they can do to resolve local problems" (p. 366). Empowering students allows them to have a personal stake in their learning. By empowering students, problem-based learning can help to improve students' attitudes. When problem-based learning instruction is created it must involve flexible lessons instead of rigid ones because students prove to be more willing to learn when they have a choice (Shin, 2006).

Several studies (Dean, 1999; Lieux, 2001; Schmidt and van der Molen, 2001; Schmidt et al., 2006) have shown that students consider PBL to be effective in promoting their learning in dealing with complex problems, enhancing their confidence in judging alternatives for solving problems, acquiring social studies content to enrich their learning of basic science information, developing thinking and problem-solving skills, improving interpersonal and professional skills, and advancing self-directed learning, higher level thinking, and enhancement of information management skills.

In sum, PBL research results overall have clearly demonstrated advantages of PBL for preparing students for real-world challenges. The emphasis of PBL curricula on application of domain knowledge, problem solving, higher order thinking, and self-directed learning skills equips students with professional and life-long learning habits of mind, which are indispensable qualities of successful professionals. Although PBL students' performance in basic domain knowledge acquisition has been slightly inferior to traditional students, the format of the tests and the time-delay effects (PBL students have been found to retain information much longer and better than traditional students) may justify this result. This speculation may suggest further research issues and merit empirical evidence to shed deeper insight on these aspects of PBL.

These submissions imply that geography students' learning through the problem-based learning method allows them to interact with geographic materials, manipulate variables and explore phenomena on the environment. Also, it equips the learners with the skills which affords them the opportunities to notice patterns, discover underlying causalities, and learn in ways that are seemingly more robust. In addition, it makes them learn better and remember easily.

Students identify their own deficiencies and progress through self-assessment

According to Pagander and Read (2014), PBL incorporates many forms of assessment, such as portfolios, self-reflection, and peer evaluation. In agreement with Pagander and Read, Tai and Yung (2007) point out that these forms of assessment are all needed to reflect the various facets of self-assessment. For example, "a portfolio allows the student to not only see the learning outcome but the learning progress as well" (Tai & Yung, 2007, p. 992). As stated in Hung et al. (2008), the ultimate goal of PBL is for students to be self-motivated, independent learners. Hence, by adopting peer review and self-assessment from group interaction, students build independence and problem-solving skills on their own. Studies (Hung et al., 2008) of the long-term benefits of PBL have shown that these skills follow students into their professional lives and give them the tools to be better prepared in terms of inter-personal skills, professional skills, and the ability to plan efficiently and independently. These findings are supported by Tai and Yung (2007) who found that authentic self-assessment better equips students to identify their own deficiencies and progress which further builds on the ideas of independent learning. Further, PBL assessment incorporates the larger concepts involved and concentrates on thinking and reasoning skills, unlike the traditional classroom settings where narrow assessment focuses on rote memory rather than true understanding (Waters & McCracken, 1997). Hence, in PBL assessment there is better understanding than the traditional lecture method. This implies that PBL assessment format may help geography students to assess their peers, identify their own deficiencies in the process and make progress.

From the above discussion on the benefits of PBL, it can be inferred that Problem-based learning improves geographic content knowledge as confirmed by studies (Brickell & Herrington, 2006; Havorson & Wescoat, 2002; Patterson et al., 2003; Tulloch & Graff, 2007). In addition, Patterson et al. (2003) opined that a high school advanced placement geography class utilizing problem-based learning resulted in students scoring significantly higher on the same test given to college undergraduates in a similar class learning under the industrialist tradition of lecture. Moreover, Problem-based learning instruction allows students to better understand more complex geographic ideas because students can relate it to their prior knowledge (Quain, 2014). Furthermore, problem-based learning with GIS improves academic achievement at younger ages and helps geography students think spatially and improve students geographic thinking skills (Bednarz, 2004; Patterson et al., 2003; Shin, 2006; Tulloch & Graff, 2007). Hence, by thinking geographically students will also start to ask questions about the world around them and then can use GIS to answer those geographic questions.

Therefore, in designing a geography curriculum, attention to students' own experiences especially pertaining to the environments in which they live must be considered (Béneker, Sanders, Tani, Taylor, & van der Vaart, 2007). Hence, it is crystal clear that PBL, as an instructional approach, is an effective medium to transmit such geographic knowledge, skills and values to geography students.

Empirical Review

This section of the literature review is devoted to reviewing empirically the works done by others which are related to or have bearing on the study. The investigator tried to come out with the similarities and more importantly, the difference between this research and earlier works. The investigator reviewed three works of other pervious researchers on the basis of their purpose of study, methodology, findings, recommendations and conclusions. The three works are:

1. Managing problem-based learning: Challenges and solutions for educational practice by Mansor, Abdullah, Wahab, Rasul, Mohd-Nor, Mohd-Nor and Raof (2015);
2. Is Problem-Based Learning (PBL) an effective teaching method? A study based on existing research by Pagander and Read (2014) and

3. Assessing students' attitudes towards geography in a problem-based learning environment by Quain (2014)

In the research of Mansor et al., (2015), the purpose of the study was to investigate the implementation of PBL in a semester in an English for Specific Purpose (ESP) class at GMI. Specific objectives were to explore the nature of problems faced by the teaching staff and students in the implementation of PBL and to identify possible solutions to the problems faced in implementing PBL. The two objectives were related to my third and fourth objectives which is the factor affecting the effective implementation of PBL and effective ways of implementing PBL instruction in geography education respectively. However, my study looks at the PBL implementation process or stages and its benefits in geography education which were not tackled by the research work under review.

In the work of Mansor et al. (2015), the study was qualitative in nature and the sample size was one (1) German-Malaysia Institute's (GMI) teaching staff or Technical Training Officer (TTO), and ten (10) students. In addition, interview and focus group interview were employed for data collection. However, this study employed mixed method and questionnaire in addition to the focus group discussion which was not used in the work under review. In addition, the sample size of the teaching staff (1) was too small for the findings to be representative of the GMI. Hence, the sample size in this study for teaching staff would be more than one to increase the reliability of this study.

According to the findings of Mansor et al., the Technical Training Officer interviewed revealed seven main categories of problems. They are challenges related to teaching of process skills, difficulty in monitoring group progress and participation, especially during self-study time, student attitude, wide array of curriculum that needs to be covered, role changes, lack of resources, especially computers and reading materials, can impede the effectiveness and understanding of PBL. Besides, the findings from the students focus group interview revealed six categories of problems related to problem interpretation, group dynamics, work overload, content acquisition, motivation, and competency levels. According to the students, their main problem lies in interpreting the problem statement. Since in PBL, they are required to explore the problem without being 'taught' any contents and learn the content while solving the problem, which unfortunately is a new concept to them. Despite the problems encountered, the students interviewed also felt that PBL is a refreshing change from the conventional method. These findings are relevant to this study since the investigator seeks to find out the factors that hinder the effective implementation of PBL in geography education.

Based on the findings of Mansor et al. (2015), it was recommended that classifying the various subjects along major themes and drafting problems based on these themes would result in further integration, thereby reducing the number of problems to be solved. In addition, integration by the thematic approach may also promote interdisciplinary and holistic understanding across subjects. Also, this may reduce the workload among teaching staff and fosters staff collaboration. Further they suggested that motivation problem can be overcome by inculcating a shared vision and a clear understanding of PBL into teaching staff, students and support staff (Aziz, 2013; Jones, Epler, Mokri, Bryant & Paretti, 2013). The objectives and benefits of PBL have to be communicated and perceived by all parties to motivate them to move towards a common goal. Moreover, curriculum-related issues such as coverage have to be evaluated continuously. As such, constant review of the curriculum and consistent monitoring of PBL classroom practices must be made a priority and must also be the norm to ensure that the educational goals of producing enterprising, employable, versatile and knowledgeable graduates are achieved. The solutions recommended are relevant to this study since the investigator seeks to find the ways of implementing PBL effectively in geography education. In spite of, the findings and the solution provided, the study failed to provide solutions to some of the problems such as lack of resources and role changes among others. Hence, this study will ensure that factors identified have solutions to it.

Pagander and Read's (2014) study sought to find empirical evidence regarding the advantages and disadvantages of PBL in the classroom and if it is appropriate for use according to the goals and guidelines set out in section 2 of GY11. Their objective, which sought to find the empirical evidence of PBL's advantages and disadvantages, is allied to this study as the investigator seeks to find the benefits and factors hindering PBL implementation in geography education.

Pagander and Read used secondary data such as publications and reports on the effectiveness of PBL and reviewed it empirically. Since it was purely secondary data, there was no sample size and the use of instrument. But this study would use primary data, notably field data, to assess the benefits and factors that hinder the effective implementation of PBL in geography.

The study revealed that students in PBL classes feel like they have learned more and are more engaged in the learning process and engagement is a common goal. In addition, the majority of the PBL research suggests that weaker students benefit from teamwork and problem solving sessions in mixed ability groups. Furthermore, it was found that PBL increases the students' problem-solving abilities and practical skills as well as contributing to an overall positive mood in both the teachers and students. Lastly, most of the PBL research reviewed by Pagander and Read. also indicated that PBL method leads to gaining life skills which are taken into the professional world such as; planning skills, independent learning skills, independent thinking skills, and reasoning skills.

Contrary to the empirical evidence supporting the advantages, Pagander and Read (2014) found that PBL method benefits stronger students who already have a good learning ethic whilst weaker students find the method challenging. Additionally, working in teams and lack of the planning skills required lead to demotivation in weaker students. Moreover, the study under review found that PBL is not suitable for sequential learning subjects, such as engineering, and needs to be adapted to meet the needs of the specific subject. This again refers to rote knowledge rather than problem-solving skills. Finally, the study revealed that the current class size makes PBL difficult. Current class sizes are too large, thus there are too many groups for the tutor to help effectively. These findings are significant to this study due to the fact the study seeks to find the benefits and the factors that affect the effective implementation of PBL in geography education.

Based on these findings, Pagander and Read conclude that PBL is a method, like all the others, which works in some situations with some students. They summarized that not enough research has been done, or really can be done due to ethical limitations, to generalize and concretely state that PBL is a method which increases knowledge retention. However, according to majority of the research, it increases the ability of many students to find answers through the development of problem-solving skills and independent thinking, increases students' engagement in their education, and promotes life skills. Inferring from the conclusion, it means that it is not in all situations and students that PBL increases knowledge retention. This is an interesting conclusion to find out in my study context.

The study of Quain (2014) sought to find out whether the introduction of problem-based learning positively improve high school students' attitude towards geography, preferences towards working in a group and problem-solving efficacy. In addition, the study sought to assess the relationship between high school students' attitudes towards geography and preference for working in groups as well as problem-solving efficacy after problem-based learning instruction. Quain's objectives are related to the second objective of this study, which is the benefits of PBL learning in geography education. Besides, it is connected to the two hypotheses of this study which seek to find out the significant difference between the effects of PBL and Lecture Method on geography students' problem solving skills and preference for group work.

Further, Quain's study was quantitative in nature with a sample size of 27 students. Also, the instrument used was the Test of Geography-Related Attitudes (ToGRA) (Walker, 2006), a valid test "to determine students' attitudes towards geography" (p.179). The study under review limited the study to only the collection of quantitative data which did not allow the researcher to collect or interpret students' observed responses to the experience, thus limited conclusions are possible from survey responses. In avoiding such limitations in this study, the investigator will mix my method at the instrumentation and data collection stage where I will use both questionnaires and focus group interview in addition to both descriptive and inferential statistics, including mean, standard deviation, skewness, correlation and t-test. Comparing the research objectives/questions, the statistical tools used by Quain (2014) were appropriate. Hence, this study will employ same statistical tools (descriptive and inferential) in analysing my data. This is because this study seeks to determine the extent of agreement between the items in research questions one to four and employ independent t-test for determining the significant effects of PBL and Lecture method on students' problem-solving skills and preference for group work.

According to the findings of Quian (2014), students' attitudes towards geography did change after the introduction of problem-based learning as the mean score from the pre-survey (M =3.00) increased during the post-survey (M =3.06) and resulted in a change of 0.06. However, the change was not statistically significant when the t-test was conducted. Also, students' preference for working in groups did not change after problem-based learning instruction. This was evident in the mean score from the pre-survey (M =3.80) to the post-survey (M =3.80).   However,   the study found that students' attitudes towards problem solving efficacy changed after the introduction of problem-based learning, as the mean score from the pre-survey (M =2.90) to the post-survey (M =3.02) had a difference of 0.12. Additionally, Quain found that there was no significant correlational relationship between geographic attitudes and preference for group work as well as problem solving efficacy before or after the course. These findings are essential to this study since the study seeks to find out the benefits of PBL instruction in geography and also, determine the significant difference between the effect of PBL and Lecture method on geography students' problem solving skills and preference for group work.

In Quain's conclusion, he indicated that lack of exposure to student-centred approaches may be a possible explanation for why the results also failed to show any change in or a correlational relationship between students' geographic attitudes, preference for group work, and problem-solving efficacy. In addition, students may have resisted the change from the teacher-centred industrialist classrooms. This explanation is consistent with Mergendoller et al. (2006) explanation that the lack of exposure to group work and problem-solving in teacher-centred classrooms may influence students' survey responses. Students may have thought about their experiences in teacher-centred classrooms when responding to survey questions about group work and problem solving.

In conclusion, the research work of Mansor et al. (2015) and Pagander and Read (2014) revealed teaching of process skills, difficulty in monitoring group progress and participation, student attitude, wide array of curriculum that needs to be covered, role changes, lack of resources, lack of the planning skills leading to demotivation in weaker students among others are some of the problems or factors that hinder the effective implementation of PBL as a method of instruction. Also, Quian (2014), found that students' attitudes towards geography, preference for group work, and problem-solving efficacy insignificantly changed with the use of problem based learning instruction. He attributed this finding to lack of exposure to student-centred approaches.

Hence, Mansor et al. suggested that various subjects should be classified along major themes and draft problems based on these themes which would reduce the number of problems to be solved. In addition, the problem of motivation can be overcome by inculcating a shared vision and a clear understanding of PBL among teaching staff and students. Likewise, objectives and benefits of PBL have to be communicated and perceived by all parties to motivate them to move towards a common goal whilst curriculum-related issues such as coverage have to be evaluated continuously.

Theoretical Framework

According to Prince and Felder (2006), the model of education that has dominated higher education for centuries (positivism), absolute knowledge (objective reality), exists independently of human perception. The teacher's job is to transmit this knowledge to the student. The natural method for this transmission is lecturing whereas and the students' job is to absorb it. However, there is an alternative theory of learning which holds that whether or not there is an objective reality, individuals actively construct and reconstruct their own reality in an effort to make sense of their experience. This is the theory of constructivism and forms the theoretical basis for this study. Though some have traced it as far back as the 4th–6th century B.C. in the works of Lao Tzu, Buddha, and Heraclitus (Prince & Felder, 2006), the constructivist view of learning is reflected in the developmental theories of Piaget (1972), Dewey (1997), Bruner (1966), and Vygotsky (1978), among others. In cognitive constructivism, Piaget pointed out that an individual's reactions to experiences lead to learning whilst in social constructivism, Vygotsky, indicated that language and interactions with others (family, peers, teachers) play a primary role in the construction of meaning from experience. Meaning is not simply constructed, it is co-constructed. Proponents of constructivism offer variations of the following principles for effective instruction:

1. Instruction should begin with content and experiences likely to be familiar to the students, so they can make connections to their existing knowledge structures. New material should be presented in the context of its intended real-

world applications and its relationship to other areas of knowledge, rather than being taught abstractly and out of context.

2. Material should not be presented in a manner that requires students to alter their cognitive models abruptly and drastically. In Vygotsky's terminology, the students should not be forced outside their "zone of proximal development," the region between what they are capable of doing independently and what they have the potential to do under adult guidance or in collaboration with more capable peers. They should also be directed to continually revisit critical concepts, improving their cognitive models with each visit. As Bruner puts it, instruction should be "spirally organized."

3. Instruction should require students to fill in gaps and extrapolate material presented by the instructor. The goal should be to wean the students away from dependence on instructors as primary sources of required information, helping them to become self-learners.

4. Instruction should involve students working together in small groups. This attribute, which is considered desirable in all forms of constructivism and essential in social constructivism, supports the use of collaborative and cooperative learning.

Problem-based learning is based on constructivist assumptions/ principles of learning as alluded to by Barrett (2005). PBL has a social constructivist view of learning. Furthermore, Schmidt, Rotgans and Yew (2011) pointed out that Problem-based learning addresses the need to promote lifelong learning through the process of inquiry and constructivist learning. Besides, PBL can be considered a constructivist approach to instruction, emphasizing collaborative and self-directed learning and being supported by flexible teacher-scaffolding (Schmidt, Loyens, Van-Gog & Paas, 2007). Gravett (2001) points out that when using constructivist or social constructivist approaches, the learner, rather than the teacher, is central to the learning process since the learner participates in acquiring and assimilating knowledge whilst the teacher functions as a facilitator. In agreement to Hmelo-Silver and Barrows (2006) state that PBL follows a constructivist perspective in learning as the role of the instructor is to guide and challenge the learning process rather than strictly providing knowledge. Also, students are considered to be active agents who engage in social knowledge construction. PBL assists in processes of creating meaning and building personal interpretations of the world based on experiences and interactions (Evensen & Hmelo, 2000). According to Edens (2000), PBL assists to guide the student from theory to practice in the course of their journey through solving the problem.

From the assumptions of the theory vis-à-vis the nature of Problem-based learning, it is clear that PBL is entrenched in the constructivist philosophy or theory of learning. This is because both the theory and PBL are student-centred approaches of learning where learners, out of their experiences and exploration, construct their own knowledge with or without the instructor's guidance. From this perspective, feedback and reflection on the learning process and group dynamics are essential components of PBL. Additionally, the learner is the central focus in the learning process, not the instructor. Also, the constructivist believes that the learner is not a tabula rasa as was claimed by John Locke, a belief mutually held by the PBL. Furthermore, discovery learning is one of the cardinal points of both the constructivist theory and PBL.

Therefore, PBL as an instructional approach for geography education may enable students the ability to explore and engage in geographic inquiry which will improve their geographic content knowledge as opined by Brickell and Herrington (2006); Havorson and Wescoat (2002); Tulloch and Graff (2007) among others. This is very essential due to the fact that geography deals with the study of spatial patterns, man and his relationship with his environment, processes that occur on, above and beneath the earth's surface which give rise to a phenomena or landform and requires that students observe and describe what forces influence the phenomena or how it occurs. That is why Quain (2014) indicates that geography educators do not have to look very far for an instructional strategy to best embrace a student-centred, interdisciplinary approach.

Conceptual Framework for the Study

This study presents a conceptual framework on the efficacy of PBL method in geography education in the University of Cape Coast. This framework comprises a component of activities involving a comprehensive review of the literature showing the relationships of the different key constructs that the investigator would want to investigate and a review of theoretical issues and model as well as empirical studies on how effectively PBL implementation process influences the teaching and learning of geography. Figure 1 shows the conceptual framework for the study.

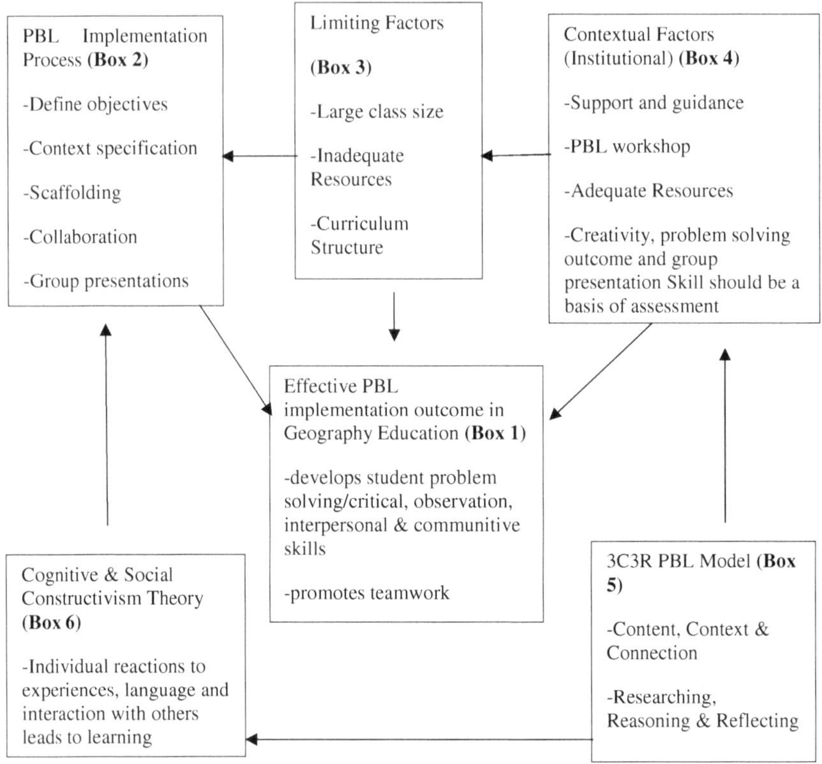

Figure 2: Conceptual Framework for the Study

Source: Investigator's Construct (Egidius ,1999; Nasr & Ramadan, 2008 Sendag & Ferhan-Odabasi, 2009)

Explanation of the conceptual framework

The conceptual framework for the study as showed in figure 2, presents the constructivists theory (box 6) whose assumptions/principles underpin the PBL method as Barret (2005) opined that PBL is based on constructivist assumptions/principles of learning. Schmidt, Loyens, Van-Gog and Paas (2007) indicate that PBL can be considered a constructivist approach to instruction, emphasising collaborative, self-directed learning and being supported by flexible teacher-scaffolding.

As presented in figure 1, the conceptual framework of the study suggests that effective implementation of PBL method in geography consists of inter-related set of elements. For instance, the effective PBL implementation process is affected or influenced by certain limiting factors (box 3) such as large class size, inadequate resources, curriculum structure (traditional system of assessment and teaching [lecture] of a course) etc. These factors negatively affect the effective implementation of PBL in geography as Egidius (1999) indicated that one of the major problems teachers face using PBL method is large classroom sizes. Studies have shown that due to large numbers of students in a class, instructors had to divide the class into several small groups and guide all of them at the same time posing difficulties for instructors to monitor each group's progress and problem (Egidius ,1999; Nasr & Ramadan, 2008).

Hence, the framework suggests that contextual factors (Institutional) (box 4) such as support and guidance from administrators, PBL workshop or seminars for lecturers and students, and restructuring the assessment system to focus on PBL ideas of assessment would help to remedy the limiting factors to ensure effective use of PBL which would result in the realisation of the benefits the method offers in its use as studies have revealed that PBL promotes the development of critical thinking, observation, problem solving, interpersonal skills, teamwork and lifelong learning [box 1] (Sendag & Ferhan-Odabasi, 2009; Benson, 2003; Vernon, 1995).

Furthermore, the 3C3R problem designing model (box 5) conceptualized by Hung (2006a) suggests some critical elements to aid the PBL implementation process in designing effective PBL problem. The 3C3R stands for content, context, connection and researching, reasoning and reflecting respectively. This model ensures the appropriateness and sufficiency of content knowledge, knowledge contextualization and its integration in order to promote students' acquisition of content knowledge and the development of problem-solving skills and self-directed learning skills.

In summary, it can be said that factors such large class size, inadequate resources and curriculum structure influence the effective implementation of PBL in Geography. Therefore, to make PBL method effective in geography education, there should be provision of support and guidance from administrators of the institution, PBL workshops and adoption of the suggestions of Hung's (2006a) 3C3R model for effective PBL implementation in geography education.

Summary of Chapter

This chapter covered the theoretical, conceptual framework and empirical review of Problem-based learning implementation in geography education. The theoretical review focused on the constructivists' theory and philosophy of learning, which holds that individuals actively construct and reconstruct their own reality in an effort to make sense of their experience. This theory underpinned PBL method because both the theory and PBL are student-centred approaches to learning where learners, out of their experiences and exploration, construct their own knowledge with or without the instructor's guidance. In addition, Hung (2006a) 3C3R PBL problem design model which is a systematic method specifically designed to guide instructional designers and educators to design effective PBL problems for all levels and across disciplines of learners was adopted to aid the study.

Literature was reviewed on the concept, characteristics and the process involved in the implementation of PBL. Mayer (2013) described PBL to consist of a multi-phased collaborative approach to education where students gain knowledge as they work in small groups (3-5 students) and attempt to solve a problem carefully-designed by the instructor. In addition, some of the features of PBL are that it is problem-focused, student-centred, self-directed, self-reflective, tutors are facilitators, among others. Furthermore, Hung, Jonassen and Liu (2008), Duch (2001) and Padmavathy and Mareesh's (2013) steps or processes involved in PBL implementation were looked at.

Also, challenges affecting the effective implementation of PBL in geography education was reviewed as part of the conceptual issues. Some of the challenges include large classroom size, nature of educational system and curriculum structure; inadequate resources (time, money and logistics), traditional/convectional assumptions of the students, student assessment and the suitability of the PBL for all students, both strong and weaker students (Chakravathi & Heleagrahara, 2010; Egidius, 1999b; Mansor et al., 2015; Luk, 2002; Wee, 2000; Omoro & Nato, 2014). Additionally, ways of ensuring effective implementation of PBL method in geography education was reviewed. Some ways suggested by Mansor et al. (2015) include; subjects should be classified along major themes and draft problems based on these themes, which would reduce the number of problems to be solved. In addition, objectives and benefits of PBL have to be communicated and perceived by all parties to motivate them and curriculum-related issues such as coverage have to be appraised continuously. Besides, Genareo and Lyons' (2015) six steps and Pawson et al. (2006) best practices for effective PBL implementation was reviewed to aid the study.

Besides, literature was reviewed on the benefits of PBL in geography education. Studies (Brickell & Herrington, 2006; Havorson & Wescoat, 2002; Patterson et al., 2003; Tulloch & Graff, 2007) revealed that Problem-based learning improves geographic content knowledge, allows students to better understand more complex geographic ideas and develops student intellectual/ analytical and problem solving skills. In addition, it promotes self-directed/life-long learning, confidence, etc. and reinforce students interpersonal and teamwork skills. Also, Patterson et al., (2003) showed that problem-based learning with Geographic Information System (GIS) helps geography students think spatially and improve students' geographic thinking skills as well as their academic achievements.

The empirical review discussed the works of Mansor et al. (2015), Pagander and Read (2014) and Quian, (2014) on issues such as the purpose/objectives of the study, the methodology, the findings and lastly the conclusion and recommendation for further research. Mansor et al. (2015) and Pagander and Read (2014) indicated teaching of process skills, difficulty in monitoring group progress and participation, wide array of curriculum that needs to be covered, lack of resources among others as the problems or factors affecting the effective implementation of PBL. Likewise, Quian (2014) found that lack of exposure to student-centred approaches contributing to students' negative attitudes towards geography, preference for group work, and problem-solving efficacy. The next chapter is the methodology which indicates the design and instrument used as well as how data was collected and analysed.

CHAPTER THREE
RESEARCH METHODS

Overview

This chapter describes how data was collected and discusses the procedures as well as techniques which was followed to conduct the study. It included research design, the target population, sample size and sampling technique, the research instrument, data collection procedures and data analysis.

Research Design

Nconco (2006) explained that a research design is the "blueprint or detailed plan for how a research study is to be conducted-operationalising variables so that they can be measured, selecting a sample of interest to study, collecting data to be used as a basis for testing hypothesis and analysing results" (p. 63). This study employed mixed methods approach. Johnson (2014) defined mixed method as the type of research in which a researcher or team of researchers mixes or combines both qualitative and quantitative research philosophies/paradigms, methodologies, methods, techniques, approaches, concepts, or language into a single research study or a set of related studies. This approach was adopted for the purposes of triangulation. Besides, the convergent parallel design under mixed method research was employed for the study. In convergent parallel design, the results or data are merged by comparing, interpreting and discussing them by stating the degree to which they converge, diverge or related (Plano-Clark & Creswell, 2011).

The justification for adopting convergent parallel design was to enable triangulation to take place. According to Johnstone (2004), triangulation involves reviewing and analysing evidence from multiple sources such that a study's findings are based on the convergences of that information. In addition, it uses different data collection methods with the view to clarifying that the data are communicating what we think they are. This strengthened the integrity of conclusions drawn from the data as Plano-Clark and Creswell (2008) indicated that triangulation increases the validity of constructs and inquiry results by counteracting or maximizing the heterogeneity of irrelevant sources of variance attributable especially to inherent method bias but also to inquirer bias and biases of inquiry context. According to Johnson and Onwuegbuzie (2004), mixed method is more expensive, time consuming and can be difficult for a single researcher to carry out both qualitative and quantitative research, especially if two or more approaches are expected to be used concurrently. In spite of the challenges, this study employed this design in order to merge both quantitative and qualitative data for discussion and interpretation to get an in-depth information about the topic under study.

Population

In every study, a researcher always has an interest in a group of people from whom he/she gathers data and draws conclusion. The larger interest group which one hopes to apply the results of a study is the population (Fraenkel & Wallen, 2006). The target population was all geography students and lecturers in the University of Cape Coast. It must be stated that the Department of Geography and Regional Planning and Department of Business and Social Sciences Education have not officially adopted the PBL method for all lecturers to use. However, instructors teaching Planning Workshop and Methods of teaching Geography employ PBL method in their instruction. Hence, the accessible population were Level 300 and 400 B.Sc. Geography and Regional Planning students reading Planning Workshop of the Department of Geography and Regional Planning, and geography education student of Department of Business and Social Sciences Education. Additionally, geography lecturers using PBL method formed part of the accessible population. In all, 186 respondents formed the population. Level 300 and 400 B.Sc. & B.Ed. geography students were used because they read courses at that level which PBL method are used. Emphasis was given to this population because the topic under study focuses on the implementation of problem-based learning method in geography education, hence geography students and lecturers who have experienced the PBL method were in the best position to provide the necessary data needed for the study.

Sample and Sampling Procedure

Preliminary data gathered from the Department of Geography and Regional Planning (DGRP), and Department of Business and Social Sciences Education (DBSSE) as well as student records office of the University of Cape Coast indicate that there are 44 level 300 and 57 level 400 B.Sc. geography students in the DGRP and 43 level 300 and 42 level 400 education geography students in the DBSSE. Hence, all the 186 geography students were included in the study. Thus, census was used to determine the participation of these students in the study. According to Harding (2013), an attempt made to collect data from every member of a population rather than choosing a sample is referred to as census. In agreement to Harding, Richard (2014) posited that a census is an attempt to gather information from each and every person of interest – the universe of the study targets. In addition, Bhanu (2011) held the view that however accurately a sample from a population may be generated, there will always be margin for error, whereas in the case of census, whole population is taken into account and as such it is most accurate. Hence, census was adopted because of the fact that the estimates are not subject to sampling error as stressed by Bhanu.

Besides, purposive sampling techniques was used to sample two (2) lecturers (one each from DGRP and DBSSE). Oliver (2006) explained that purposive sampling is a form of non-probability sampling in which decisions concerning the individuals to be included in the sample are taken by the researcher, based upon a variety of criteria which may include the respondent's specialist knowledge of the research issue, or capacity and willingness to participate in the research. The reason for adopting purposive sampling is because the research problem demands experts in the field of study (thus Geography lecturer using the PBL method in teaching) to provide the investigator with the requisite data. Hence, two lecturers were selected on purpose for this study.

Data Collection Instruments

The research instruments that were employed in the study were questionnaire and interview guide for lecturers' in-depth interview and students' focus group discussion. The use of these two instruments were to overcome the limitations associated with the use of single data collection instrument. Thus, it enabled the investigator to triangulate data to test the consistency of the findings obtained from each instrument used. Bekoe (2006) opined that triangulation in research is to test for consistency of findings obtained through different instruments. Hence, it is imperative that different instruments were used to validate the data gathered. Sidhu (as cited in Owusu & Asare-Danso, 2014) posits that a questionnaire is a form prepared and distributed to secure responses to certain questions. In addition, it is a systematic compilation of questions that are submitted to a sampling population from which information is desired. The questionnaire was used because it promises a wider coverage since researchers can approach respondents more easily and can be completed at the respondents' convenience. Though the use of questionnaire did not allow the respondents to express their views on the problem extensively; however, in line with Leedy and Ormrod's (2005) view, the questionnaire guaranteed confidentiality and anonymity of the respondents since it was generally self-reporting.

Fifty-one (35) items were on each questionnaire which was made up of both closed-ended and open-ended questions (McBurney, 2007). The questionnaire items were grouped into five sections. The Section 'A' dealt with the demographic data of the respondents while Section 'B' focused on the first research question which was on the processes or stages involved in the implementation of PBL in geography education. Section 'C' covered items on challenges affecting the effective implementation of PBL in geography. Furthermore, the third research question which was on the ways of ensuring effective implementation of PBL in geography education was covered in Section 'D'. Then Section 'E' dealt with the benefits of PBL in geography education which was the fourth research question. Apart from the demographic data which was a mixture of open and closed ended questions, Sections B to E were designed on a five-point Likert scale responses in a descending order from "Strongly Agree, Agree, Neutral, Disagree and Strongly Disagree". The Likert scale was appropriate because it is one of the most universal methods for survey collection and for that matter, is easily understood and get quick responses from respondents. In addition, the responses on the scale were easily quantifiable and good for computation of mathematical analysis as well as having high versatility which can be sent through mail or given in person (LaMarca, 2011).

Besides the questionnaire, the investigator conducted two focus group discussions for selected students from the two departments (one focus group discussion for each department) to probe further into some issues which the questionnaire was not able to provide in depth information. According to Bell (2008) and Denscombe (2008), focus group discussion is where the researcher becomes the moderator in the process to bring a number of respondents together to a convenient location to assess their views, experiences and feelings on a phenomenon. The focus group discussion questions were made up of 12 items centred on the research questions and the hypotheses. Another semi-structured interview guide was used to conduct in-depth interview for two lecturers. This was done in order to have much information and broader overview of the topic under study to draw informed conclusions. Conferring to Twumasi (2001), interview provides the interviewer the flexibility and certain confidential information which might not have obtained from using questionnaires. To Kumekpor (2002), an interview affords the interviewer the opportunity to explain the purpose of the investigation and can explain more clearly just what information he/she wants. He further indicates that "if the subject misinterprets the question, the interviewer may follow up with a clarifying question" (p.29). The semi-interview guide questions for the lecturers' interview consisted of ten (10) items designed according to the research questions and hypotheses. The adoption of these methods enabled the investigator to meet with the geography lectures' and students to express their views on the topic under study. In addition, it enabled the investigator to seek more clarification on issues which the questionnaire could not.

Validity and Reliability of Instrument

The research instruments were subjected to a validity and reliability test. Validity refers to the degree to which evidence and theory supports the interpretations of test scores entailed by proposed uses of tests (Ary, Jacobs, Razavieh & Sorensen,

2006). It deals with the appropriateness and the usefulness of the results while reliability refers to the degree of consistency to which the instruments can yield comparable results. The face and content validity of the questionnaire and the interview guide questions were determined through expert judgement by the investigator's supervisors and colleague researchers. The face validity ensured that the questions were clear, relevant and unambiguous for the respondents (Ary et al., 2006) while the content validity judged the extent to which the content of an instrument appears logical in examining the full scope of the domains it intends to measure (Bowling, 2002). The suggestions given by the supervisors or experts were used to effect the necessary changes to improve upon the validity of the instrument.

Thereafter, a pilot test of the instruments was conducted on Level 200 geography students of the Department of Business and Social Sciences Education to pave way for feedback on the completeness and the appropriateness of the items in both instruments. The completed questionnaires were collected, edited for completeness, coded and analysed with the aid of computer software known as IBM Statistical Product for Service Solution (SPSS Version 22). Cronbach co-efficient alpha was established for each item in the questionnaires to determine their reliability. Thus, the reliability co-efficient of items under research question one was .88 while for research question two was .73. Additionally, items under research question three had a reliability co-efficient of .71 and the fourth research question obtained .82 as the reliability co-efficient. Since, Cohen, Manion and Morrison (2007) pointed that a reliability co-efficient of .70 is considered high and therefore adequate and the overall reliability of the instrument was .88, it was considered sufficiently reliable and adequate.

Data Collection Procedure

The survey was carried out by the investigator himself in both departments (DGRP & DBSSE). This was done from the 20th March to 17th April, 2017. A letter of introduction was obtained from the Department of Business and Social Sciences Education, University of Cape Coast, this enabled the investigator to obtain permission from the postgraduate Coordinator of Department of Geography and Regional Planning who also happens to be one of the instructors teaching planning workshop course. After my briefing with the instructor about what the study is about, he then introduced the investigator to the class. The respondents were briefed as to what the study was about in order to get their understanding, attention, support and co-operation for the data collection. In addition, the respondents were assured of their confidentiality and they were given 30 minutes to fill or answer the questionnaire. The investigator retrieved 170 questionnaires and had a return rate of (91%). According to Dilman (2000), return rate from seventy percent (70%) is classified as a good and acceptable return rate. This return rate was due to the fact that within the one and half month data collection and follow ups, there was no day the investigator met a full class. The situation was confirmed by the class attendance list for the course the investigator had to go through.

After filling the questionnaire, eight (8) each of the same students from DGRP and DBBE were selected for two different focus group discussion. Prior information was given so as to prepare their minds for the exercise. The focus group discussions for both departments took place on 20th and 21st April, 2017 respectively with each discussion lasting for about 45 minutes. Also, the lecturers' interview was done from 24th -25th April, 2017. One of the lecturer's (B.Sc. instructor) interview lasted for 26 minutes while the other lecturer's (B.Ed. instructor) lasted for 23 minutes. A tape recorder was used to record the responses of the discussions and the lecturers' interview. Some of the responses were written on a paper.

Ethical Considerations

Ethical issues concerning the right and confidentiality of the prospective respondents were addressed by the investigator, in order not to be accused of infringing upon the rights and privacy of the respondents. Firstly, the informed consent of the prospective respondents was sought to participate in the field study and provide them with an explanation of the purposes of the study and expected duration of their participation. Also, steps were taken to protect or prevent risk or harm to participants. For example, issues of embarrassment were presented by not disclosing their identities or not informing third party of the discussions.   Confidentiality   – thus, withholding real names and other identifying characteristics of respondents. The right of the respondents to veto the research results was upheld. Additionally, respect was accorded participants as subjects and not as objects to be used and then discarded. Participants were given a statement that participation is voluntary, refusal to participate involved no penalty or loss of benefits to which the participants were otherwise entitled, and the participant may discontinue at any time without penalty or loss of benefits to which the participants was otherwise entitled. Soft copies of the research report were sent to the instructors of the departments involved in the study.

Data Processing and Analysis

Since the study used mixed method in data collection, this technique was also employed in the analysis stage. For the quantitative data, it was sorted, edited, coded and analysed. The editing of the questionnaires helped to remove uncompleted questionnaires while the coding aided in assigning numerals to the various responses of the items on the questionnaire and the Likert scale type of responses. The data was analysed using the IBM SPSS (version 22). In this study, both descriptive statistical tools were used in analysing the data into frequencies and percentages, means and standard deviations. The reason for using means and standards deviation was to enable the investigator to find the extent of agreements on the processes or stages involved in PBL implementation in geography; challenges affecting it effective implementation; ways to ensure it effective implementation in geography and the benefits of PBL in teaching geography. Besides, the data recorded from the focus group discussion was transcribed. Creswell (2008) notes that "transcription is the process of converting audiotape recordings or field notes into text data" (p. 246). Additionally, the text data was generated in pre-set themes according to the research questions/hypotheses and discussed. Pre-set themes are themes generated before the analysis of the recorded data (Kusi, 2012).

Summary of Chapter

The mixed method approach specifically the Convergent parallel design was employed for the study. Level 300 and 400 B.Sc. Geography and Regional Planning students and B.Ed. Social Sciences students (Geography Major) as well as lecturers formed the accessible population for the study. Census and Purposive sampling techniques were adopted and questionnaire as well as interview guide were used to gather data from respondents. On the collection of data, an introductory letter was obtained from the Department of Business and Social Sciences Education which enabled the investigator to obtain permission from the Head of Department of the DGRP and the lecturers that were interviewed. SPSS version 22 was used to analyse the quantitative data while thematic analysis was adopted for the qualitative analysis. The next chapter which is chapter four dealt with the presentation and discussion of the data obtained.

CHAPTER FOUR

RESULTS AND DISCUSSION

Overview

The purpose of this study was to investigate the efficacy of Problem-Based Learning method in Geography Education in the University of Cape Coast of the Central Region. Questionnaire which contained 35 items was employed for the study and these items were measured on a five-point Likert scale (SA, A, NS, D, SD). In addition, an interview guide which contained 12 items was used for the interview of the key informant (lecturer) and the students focus group discussion. Census was adopted to involve all level 300 and 400 B.Sc. and B.Ed. Geography students in the study. Descriptive statistics and Thematic analysis were used to analyse the data. This chapter deals with the presentation and discussion of the findings of the study. The findings were organized and presented in line with the research questions of the study. The chapter is divided into two sections. The first section focused on the demographic data of the respondents whilst the second aspect concentrated on the presentation and discussion of the main findings of the study.

Demographic Data of the Respondents

This section discusses the information collected on the demographic background of the respondents. The purpose for the discussion of the demographic characteristics of the respondents is to show that the right respondents who had relevant experience in the subject area were used. The characteristics of the respondents discussed here include the department, programme pursued, level of education and gender. Table 1 presents the demographic data of the respondents.

Table 1 - Demographic Data of Respondents

Variable	Sub-scale	N	%
Department	Dept. of Geography and Regional Planning	87	51.2
	Dept. of Business and Social Sciences Education	83	48.8
Programme	B.Sc. Geography and Regional Planning	87	51.2
	B. Ed. Social Sciences (Geography Major)	83	48.8
Level	300	85	50.0
	400	85	50.0
Gender	Male	109	64.1
	Female	61	35.9

Source: Field survey, Bentil (2017)

From the results in Table 1, 87(51.2%) of the respondents were from the Department of Geography and Regional Planning [DGRP] whilst 83(48.8%) of the respondents were from the Department of Business and Social Sciences Education [DBSSE]. On the programme that the respondents were reading, the results found that 87(51.2%) of the respondents were reading B.Sc. Geography and Regional Planning and 83(48.8%) were reading B.Ed. Social Sciences (Geography Major). This implies that majority of the respondents involved in the study were from DGRP and reading B.Sc. Geography and Regional Planning. This difference could be attributed to the fact that the number of level 300 and 400 students reading B.Sc. Geography and Regional Planning from the DGRP was more than respondents reading B.Ed. Social Sciences from the DBSSE.

Regarding the level of education of the respondents, it was revealed that 85(50.0%) were level 300 students and 85(50.0%) were level 400 students. This means that there was equal representation of both level 300 and 400 student respondents in the study. Concerning the gender of the respondents, it was found that 109(64.1%) of the respondents were males whilst 61(35.9) were females. This denotes that most of the respondents involved in the study were males. This difference could be ascribed to the fact that there are more males than females in both departments reading B.Sc. Geography and Regional Planning as well as B.Ed. Social Sciences (Geography Major) and in the University of Cape Coast at large.

Discussion of Main Results

This part of the study covers the main findings that emerged from the study. The results are organized and discussed in accordance with the research questions guiding the study. This was done to ensure achievement of the various research questions set at the beginning of the study and to provide well organised discussions to enhance easy understanding of the findings of the study. The findings of the two hypotheses underlying the study are also discussed under this part. Since, descriptive statistics such as mean and standard deviation were used in analysing the data, the decision rule that was followed is presented in the Table 2 and 3.

Table 2 - Decision Rule for Means Values

Mean	Scale
5.0-4.5	SA
4.4-3.5	A
3.4-3.0	NS
2.9-2.5	D
2.4-1.0	SD

Source: Field survey, Bentil (2017)

From Table 2, the analysis and discussion of the study's finding using the mean values followed this interval. The responses between 1.0 – 2.4 were concluded to be Strongly Disagree, 2.5 – 2.9 to be Disagree whilst 3.0 – 3.4 denoted Not Sure.

Additionally, 3.5 – 4.4 signified Agreed whilst 4.5 – 5.0 indicated Strongly Agreed. With respect to the standard deviation, the following decision rules were used to guide the study. Table 3 represents the decision for the standard deviation.

Table 3 - Decision Rule for Standard Deviation Values

Standard Deviation Values	Interpretation
1 or greater than 1	Responses differ much from one another (Heterogeneous Responses)
Less than 1	Responses did not differ much from one another (Homogeneous Responses)

Source: Field survey, Bentil (2017)

From Table 3, when the standard deviation is less than 1, then it means the responses are homogenous, thus responses did not differ much from one another. However, in case the standard deviation is equal to 1 or greater than 1, then there is a heterogeneous response, meaning, the responses differ much from one another.

Research Question 1: What are the processes or stages involved in the implementation of problem-based learning in geography education?

Research question one sought to find out from the respondents their views on the processes or stages involved in implementing problem-based learning method in geography education. Items 5 to 12 under section B of the students' questionnaire and focus group discussion questions were designed to assist in finding answers to this research question. Table 4 presents the results of the processes or stages involved in the implementation of problem-based learning in geography education.

Table 4 - Processes or Stages Involved in PBL Implementation in Geography

Statement	Mean	Std. Deviation
Preamble: The instructor………………		
Defines or presents the PBL problem to students to solve.	4.26	0.796
Specifies the context in which the problem should be solved.	4.28	0.792
Guides students' to form groups to work on a particular problem in PBL implementation process.	4.38	0.722
Organises brainstorming sessions with groups before students start solving the problem.	4.00	1.049
Guides students/groups to give regular reports on	4.04	0.996

the problem solving process.

Serves as a facilitator providing guidelines for students in the PBL process.	4.21	0.791
Guides students to individually assume responsibility in the PBL implementation process.	4.06	0.918
Guides students/groups to evaluate their own learning in the PBL implementation process.	4.04	1.040
Total	4.15	0.604

Source: Field survey, Bentil (2017) Scale: SA=5, A=4, NS=3, D=2, SD=1.

From the results in Table 4, it showed that majority of the respondents agreed that their instructor defines or presents the problem-based learning (PBL) problem to them to solve and their responses did not differ much from one another. This is evident from the computed values of mean and standard deviation as 4.26 and 0.79 respectively. This confirms the finding of Padmavathy and Mareesh (2013) who indicated in their seven steps of problem based learning that the problem should be defined. On the respondents' responses to the second statement, the results showed a mean value of 4.28 and a standard deviation value of 0.79. This implies that majority of the respondents agreed that their instructor specifies the context in which the problem should be solved and their responses were homogeneous. However, the results from the focus group discussion (FGD) showed otherwise. For instance, the students remarked:

"With respect to objective and context specification, some lecturers do while others do not. Some just tell us to research on a topic of our choice and come and present in class while others give us a specific topic and tell us to research on it and present in class. The difference is that, those who give the topic normally do not specify the objectives but in some cases some specify the objective(s). The education lecturer always gives us the objectives" (FGD with B.Ed. Students, 20th April, 2017).

Although there was some disagreement on the extent to which instructors provide guidance to structure the context and objectives of the PBL but it was observed that in general the lecturers were doing well with context specification of PBL. These findings are in line with the views of Hung (2006b) who opined in his nine-step problem design process that context specification analysis should be done by the instructor. In addition, Hung (2006a) in his 3R3C problem designing model pointed context (knowledge contextualisation) as one of the core components of the model.

Furthermore, majority of the respondents agreed that their instructor guides them to form groups to work on a particular problem in PBL implementation process and their responses were homogeneous. This is seen from a computed mean of 4.38 and standard deviation of 0.72 in Table 4. Similar finding came up from the focus group discussions with students offering B.Ed. Social Sciences (Geography Major) and B.Sc. Geography and Regional Planning. For instance, in one of the focus group discussions, the students said this:

"We are normally given the chance to form our own groups with the lecturer limiting us to a specific number of students in each group. For example, the lecturer will say form a group of five members. And we are also allowed to choose our own members" (FGD with B.Sc. Students, 21st April, 2017).

This finding is critical as it promotes teamwork and enable students to think together to address a given problem as Hung, Jonassen and Liu (2008) indicated that in PBL designing process, organising students in groups of five to eight helps them to come together and reason through a problem. It further corresponds with Genareo and Lyons' (2015) observation that PBL research should begin with small-group which encourage brainstorming among students about a given problem and in terms of sharing ideas about what they know about the problem and the issues to be studied.

On the statement of whether the instructor organises brainstorming sessions with groups before students start solving the problem, the results found a mean of 4.00 and standard deviation of 1.04. This implies that majority of the respondents agreed to the statement but their responses were heterogeneous thus differ much from one another. This difference in their responses could be attributed to that fact that the instructors do not always organise brainstorming sessions for students before they start the problem solving process. This confirms the finding of the focus group discussion in which one of the students remarked as follows:

"Our lecturer organises brainstorming sessions for us before we start the problem solving process but it is not always that our lecturer organises brainstorming sessions for us before the start of the problem solving process" (FGD with B.Ed. Students 20th April, 2017).

This finding is in consonance with the observation by Briggs (2015) that the first few class meetings in a PBL course should include brainstorming sessions in which issues central to the course are identified for students to know what they are expected to do in the problem solving process. In relation to the students' responses on the statement that "their instructor guides students/groups to give regular reports on the problem solving process", most of the students agreed to this statement and their responses were homogenous as the computed mean value was 4.04 and standard deviation value was 0.99. This finding supports Duch's (2001) view that the class time may be devoted to groups reporting out their progress on previous learning issues and listing their current learning issues as well as plans of work.

The results also revealed that the instructor serves as a facilitator providing guidelines for students in PBL process and their responses did not differ much from one another as the computed mean value was 4.21 and standard deviation was 0.79. This discovery is in line with the finding of Hung et al. (2008) who connoted that tutors are facilitators who support and model reasoning processes, facilitate group processes, probe students' knowledge deeply and never interject content or provide direct answers to questions. It further affirms Dahlgren's (2003) assertion that instructors act as facilitators rather than primary sources of information in the problem–based learning process.

Furthermore, majority of the respondents agreed that their instructor guides students/groups to evaluate their own learning in the PBL implementation but their responses differ much from one another as the computed mean value and standard deviation were 4.04 and 1.04 respectively. This finding endorse's Padmavathy and Mareesh's (2013) revelation that students report and evaluate on self-directed learning in their group meeting. The overall results of the processes or stages involved in the implementation of PBL method in geography education had a mean value and standard deviation of 4.15 and 0.60 respectively. It can be deduced that majority of the respondents agreed to the statements that sought their responses on the processes involved in implementation of PBL in geography education and their responses were generally homogenous. Linking it to the conceptual framework, it implies that the students will enjoy the benefits or outcomes of the PBL implementation in geography which will make the students develop positive attitude towards the course.

Research Question 2: What are the challenges affecting the effective implementation of problem-based learning method in geography education?

Research question two sought to assess the respondents' opinion on the challenges that affect the effective implementation of problem-based learning method in geography education. Items 13 to 20 under section C of the student's questionnaire were designed to assist in finding answers to this research question. The results are presented in Table 5.

Table 5 - Challenges Affecting the Effective Implementation of PBL in Geography

Statement	Mean	Std. Deviation
Large class size negatively affects the effective use of PBL in geography.	4.36	0.953
Instructors have difficulty in maintaining the effectiveness of learning with large numbers of groups in a class.	4.22	0.880
The loaded nature of the geography curriculum makes it difficult to use PBL method in teaching.	4.11	0.955
The traditional assessment (examination) system affects the use of PBL in geography.	3.98	1.020
PBL method is time consuming and that makes it difficult to be used effectively in geography.	3.84	1.143
Inadequate logistics affects the effective use of PBL method in geography.	4.39	0.772
The expensive nature of the PBL method makes it difficult to be implemented effectively.	4.05	0.937
The conventional teaching method (Lecture) where students look up to the instructor for knowledge affects the use of PBL.	3.86	1.158
Total	4.10	0.522

Source: Field survey, Bentil (2017) Scale: SA=5, A=4, NS=3, D=2, SD=1.

From the results in Table 5, majority of the respondents agreed that large class size negatively affect the effective use of PBL in geography and their responses did not differ much from one another (M= 4.36, SD= 0.95). This finding corresponds with Egidius's (1999) assertion that one of the major problems a teacher faces using the PBL method is large classroom size. He explained that due to the number of students in a class, there are very few classes in which one can conduct a PBL session. In addition, Bonwell (1998) revealed that large class sizes are too big to permit the use of PBL method. The results further showed that most of the respondents agreed that instructors have difficulty in maintaining the effectiveness of learning with large numbers of groups in class and their responses were homogeneous (M= 4.22, SD= 0.88). This finding is very crucial as it hinders the effectiveness of the use of the PBL method and therefore affecting the realisation of PBL, its beauty and benefits as Luk (2004) opined that instructors have difficulty in maintaining and guaranteeing the effectiveness of learning with large numbers of groups in a class.

Furthermore, the results depicted that majority of the respondents agreed that the loaded nature of the geography curriculum makes it difficult to use PBL method in teaching and their responses were homogeneous (M= 4.11, SD= 0.95). This result affirms the views of Bonwell (1998) who pointed that due to imposed accountability, the structure of the curriculum and the education system make it difficult for PBL method to be used effectively. On the statement of the traditional assessment (examination) system affects the use of PBL in geography (Table 5), the respondents agreed to the statement but their responses were heterogeneous (M= 3.98, SD= 1.02). These differences in their responses could be attributed to the fact the B.Ed. Geography Education students write exams at the end of the semester whilst the B.Sc. Geography and Regional Planning Students do not write exams at end of the semester. This finding support Wee's (2000) assertion that the traditional assessment system did not aid the effective implementation of PBL method.

Moreover, the respondents agreed that the PBL method is time consuming and that makes it difficult to be used effectively in geography but their responses differ from each other (M= 3.84, SD= 1.14). This might be as a result of the fact that different tutors handle the B.Sc. and B.Ed. Geography students and their teaching approaches may differ. For instance, the Level 300 and 400 B.Sc. Geography students work on a given problem throughout a whole year without writing exams in the course that PBL method is used as a teaching approach whilst the B.Ed. Geography students as part of the PBL method write exams at the end of the semester. The differences in responses on time consuming as a factor affecting PBL method did not only emerge from the students but also among the instructors that were interviewed. Whilst an instructor for students offering B.Ed. Social Science (Geography Major) found PBL method as time consuming, an instructor for students reading B.Sc. Geography had different views. For example, the instructor for B.Sc. Geography and Regional Planning students had this to say:

"Time factor is not a problem because they do it for a whole year. The problem has to do mainly with large numbers and not the orientation given on PBL. Basically, PBL goes with smaller numbers and resources. Per my experience, it is better to work with smaller numbers as some students play truancy and do not participate in the PBL in larger groups. Considerably, 30 members in a class/group are ok, because controlling them will be easier as compared to larger groups. Our inability to embark on more field trips is due to large numbers. Inadequate resources (e.g. Finance constraints) also impede organization of more field trips" (Instructor, 25th April, 2017)

This finding indicates that time consuming nature of PBL method is relative depending upon the extent and the course structure to which PBL method is used.

Therefore, this finding from students' respondents and B.Ed. instructor supports Luk's (2004) opinion that teachers found PBL to be time consuming which meant that they have to sacrifice their own free time to cater for students' needs whilst it conflicts the B.Sc. instructor's assertion.

Following the results in Table 5, majority of the respondents agreed that inadequate logistics affects the effective use of the PBL method in geography and their responses did not differ much from one another (M= 4.39, SD= 0.77). This finding was evident in the interview with the instructors who revealed that inadequate resources impede the organisation of field trip in the PBL process. This finding supports the observations of Omoro and Nato (2014) who opined that there are high costs associated with PBL implementation process especially when many students are to travel to distant places to study a given phenomenon. This makes PBL a very costly method to be used by teachers in teaching geography since the subject by nature require many fieldtrips. In agreement with this finding, Keller (2002), Massa, Dischino, Donnelly, Hanes and DeLaura (2012) advised that due to lack of instructional tools and models for PBL, those seeking to use and extend the use of this pedagogical method have to develop innovative curriculum, give the educators good training and provide enough resources to supports the PBL process.

Owing to the statement that conventional teaching method (lecture) where students look up to the instructor for knowledge affects the use of PBL, the respondents agreed to the statement but their responses differ from one another (M= 3.86, SD= 1.15). This could be due to the fact that majority of the respondents (Students) are used to the lecture method than the PBL method and their orientation about it may have contributed to their differences in responses as Reithlingshoefer (1992) stressed that one of the factors affecting the effective use of Problem-based learning is the traditional assumption of students that their teachers are the main disseminator of knowledge. In addition, Wee (2000) found that some of students see the PBL curriculum as confusing, uncertain and ambiguous and therefore prefers the conventional teaching methods, where they look up to their teacher as content provider and endorser of knowledge. Hence, this might be a probable reason for the difference in the students' responses on the conventional teaching method (lecture) as a factor that affect PBL discussed above.

The overall responses on the factors that affect the effective implementation of PBL method in geography had a mean and standard deviation of 4.10 and 0.52 respectively. Hence, it can be inferred that majority of the respondents agreed that above discussed challenges negatively affect the effective implementation of PBL method in geography thereby affect the benefits of its implementation as indicated by the conceptual framework of this study.

Research Question 3: What are the ways for ensuring effective implementation of problem-based learning method in geography education?

This research question was to find out from the respondents, the ways for ensuring the effective implementation of problem-based learning method in geography education. Items 21 to 27 under section D of the students' questionnaire were designed to assist in finding answers to this research question. The results are presented in Table 6.

Table 6 - Ways of Ensuring Effective Implementation of PBL in Geography

Statement	Mean	Std. Deviation
Curriculum based on PBL ideas needs to be used by the department.	4.48	0.715
Time allocation for geography courses should be increased for effective implementation of PBL.	4.06	1.177
The department should provide support and guidance for students and instructors on the use of PBL method.	4.48	0.681
Regular reports should be given by students during the PBL implementation process.	4.48	0.655
Instructors should provide clear guidelines and explanation of what students should do in the PBL process.	4.59	0.561
Instructors should hold class discussion with various groups of students before they start solving the problem given them.	4.55	0.653
Assessment of students in PBL should focus on students' creativity and problem solving outcome.	4.52	0.707
Total	4.45	0.407

Source: Field survey, Bentil (2017) Scale: SA=5, A=4, NS=3, D=2, SD=1.

The results in Table 6revealed that most of the respondents agreed that curriculum based on PBL ideas needs to be used by the department and their responses were homogeneous (M= 4.48, SD= 0.71). This finding affirms what Poikela and Poikela (2005) said "that to be able to use PBL as a teaching method, the curriculum must provide goals and guidelines according to this method, thus a curriculum based on the ideas of PBL needs to be used by the school, with the result that the entire school works with PBL method and not separate classes" (p. 58).

Besides, on the statement of time allocation for geography courses should be increased for effective implementation of PBL (Table 6), the respondents agreed to the statement but their responses differ from one another (M= 4.06, SD= 1.17). These differences in the responses could be attributed to the fact that B.Sc. Geography students work on a given problem throughout a whole year while the B.Ed. Geography students' work on a similar problem within some months or semester in the PBL process. In this case, the B.Ed. students may ask for increment in time allocation for geography courses while B.Sc. students may be okay with the duration. This results corresponds to the finding of Grimwade (2000) who warned that unless more teaching time is allocated to geography, there is the danger that geography's subject integrity will be compromised and that could affect the long term visibility of the subject. In addition, Keller (2002) opined that students needed additional time in class because they often struggled to find time outside of class for group work, a common element of PBL.

Similarly, majority of the respondents agreed that the department should provide support and guidance for students and instructors on the use of PBL method and their responses did not differ much from one another. This is evident from the computed values of mean and standard deviation of 4.48 and 0.68 respectively in Table 6. This finding is very significant since PBL method is time consuming and expensive in nature so the departments must make conscious effort to support PBL process with the available resources (be it financial, material or human resources) as Rogers (2014) pointed that the adoption and continued use of PBL requires supports and guidance for students and instructors. He explained that these support and guidance are needed from administration, to enable instructors go through PBL professional development.

Following the results from Table 6, most of the respondents strongly agreed that instructors should provide clear guidelines and explanation of what students should do in the PBL process and their responses were homogeneous (M= 4.59, SD= 0.561). Similar finding came up from the focus group discussion with both B.Ed. Social Sciences (Geography major) and B.Sc. Geography and Regional Planning students. The students said this:

"Objective should be clearly stated as in methods of teaching geography. Students should be guided on how to look for information on topics given so as to know what to include and what to exclude from the work. Students should be given much orientation on PBL especially its benefits before lecturers apply it because students focus on an exercise when they know what they will gain from it. PBL problems/questions should be clearer and free from ambiguity for easy understanding. Also enough time should be given to enable students do

effective research on the problem given" (FGD with B.Sc. Students, 21st April, 2017).

This finding is in harmony with Rogers (2014) opinion that instructors need to be explicit with students through clear guidelines and provide a thorough explanation of what will be expected of them, before PBL implementation begins. Moreover, the respondents strongly agreed that instructors should hold class discussion with various groups of students before they start solving the problem given them and their responses did not differ much from one another. This is evident from the computed values of mean and standard deviation as 4.55 and 0.65 respectively (Table 6). This finding is consistent with the opinion of Briggs (2015) who stressed that instructors should allow time for class discussion of the problem at the beginning of the class period or the end of the PBL session.

In relation to the statement on assessment of students in PBL should focus on students' creativity and problem solving outcome, most of the respondents strongly agreed to the statement and their responses were homogeneous (M= 4.52, SD= 0.70). In the same vein, the interview with an instructor for B.Sc. students reading Geography and Regional Planning also affirmed the students' findings of the assessment system. The instructor remarked:

"Yes, it is better we practically apply the PBL with less emphasis on theory. They do not write exams. But normally we do technical report writing where every member of a group is expected to take part in the work and in the classroom presentation. Also, they do oral presentation where we ask each member questions as personal assessment after they have presented. Their assessment is therefore based on these two" (Instructor, 25th April, 2017).

This finding is very essential as it promotes students' group presentation, report writing and communication skills as well as given students the opportunity to evaluate or assess their colleagues. This assessment helps to improve students' creativity, problem solving skills and presentation skills which are the core aim of PBL method. That is why Tiangco (as cited in Tai & Yuen, 2007) said that "the assessment phase in PBL process should focus on evaluating acts of creativity, problem-solving, self-management and teamwork" (p. 5). The overall responses on the ways of ensuring effective implementation of PBL method in geography had a mean and standard deviation values of 4.45 and 0.40 respectively. It can be inferred that majority of the respondents agreed that the ways discussed will ensure that the challenges affecting PBL implementation are curtailed and ensure it maximum benefits its implementation in geography education as indicated in the conceptual framework.

Research Question 4: What are the benefits of effective implementation of the problem-based learning method in geography education?

Research question four sought to find out from the respondents, the benefits that result from the effective implementation of the problem-based learning method in geography education. Items 28 to 35 under section E of the students' questionnaire were designed to assist in finding answers to this research question. The result of the benefits that result from the effective implementation of problem-based learning in geography education is represented in Table 7.

Table 7 - Benefits of Effective Implementation of PBL in Geography Education

Statement	Mean	Std. Deviation
Preamble: PBL………………..		
Develops student intellectual/critical thinking skills.	5.04	3.883
Develops student observation and problem solving skills.	4.66	0.473
Promotes students' self-directed and life-long learning.	4.55	0.596
Nurtures the leadership qualities in students.	4.45	0.738
Reinforces student communication and interpersonal skills.	4.59	0.620
Promotes teamwork among students' groups.	4.63	0.584
Develops students' confidence and attitude towards geography positively.	4.49	0.732
Helps students to identify their own deficiencies and progress through self-assessment.	4.42	0.660
Total	4.60	0.619

Source: Field survey, Bentil (2017) Scale: SA=5, A=4, NS=3, D=2, SD=1.

From Table 7, the results showed that most of the respondents strongly agreed that problem-based learning (PBL) develops student intellectual/critical thinking skills and their responses differ much from one another. This is evident from the computed values of mean and standard deviation of 5.04 and 3.88 respectively. The difference in their responses could be due to the fact that some of respondents (especially the B.Ed. students) have realised the full benefits because the limited time they work on the problem and tradition assessment system. This discovery is in consonance with the finding of Sendag and Ferhan-Odabasi (2009) who indicated that problem-based learning method can promote the development of critical thinking/ intellectual skills. Likewise, most of the respondents strongly agreed that PBL develops students' observation and problem solving skills and their responses did not differ from one another as the computed mean value was 4.66 and the standard deviation value was 0.47. This finding is critical to the development of students with requisite skills and knowledge to solve societal and national problem. It is in line with the observation of Hung et al. (2008) who revealed that one of the essential promises of PBL is improving students' problem-solving skills.

In relation to the statement that PBL promotes students' self-directed and life-long learning, majority of the respondents strongly agreed to the statement and their responses were homogeneous (M= 4.55, SD= 0.59). The finding affirms the revelation of Schmidt, Rotgans and Yew (2011) that PBL addresses the need to promote lifelong learning through the process of inquiry and constructivist learning. Furthermore, the results in Table 7 depicted that, majority of the respondents agreed that PBL nurtures the leadership qualities in students and their responses did not differ much from one another (M= 4.45, SD= 0.73). This is in agreement with the finding of Tricia and Moore (2007) that problem-based learning nurtures the leadership qualities in students, teaches them to make decision by consensus and gives constructive feedback to team members.

Following the results in Table 7, majority of the respondents strongly agreed that PBL reinforces student communication and interpersonal skills and their responses were homogeneous concerning the statement. This is evident from the computed mean and standard deviation values of 4.59 and 0.62 respectively. Owing to the statement that PBL promotes teamwork among student groups, the results showed a computed mean value of 4.63 and a standard deviation value of 0.58. This denotes that most of the respondents strongly agreed that problem-based learning promotes teamwork among student groups and their responses did not differ much from one another. Similar findings came up from the focus group discussions organised for both B.Ed. and B.Sc. geography students. For example, B.Ed. Geography students said this:

"PBL is the best because it involves group participation; it enables students to be sociable. It will help students to appreciate what they experience in the real world by knowing the causes of phenomena. It is a way of learning from others and also getting diverse information to analyse as each member of the group may have different information to share. It helps in teaming up when one goes to the field and the group teams up to provide ideas or solution to a problem. It

makes students reach the highest taxonomy as the problem-based questions that are given to students sometimes require them to think critically, criticize, analyse and synthesize the problem" (FGD B.Ed. Students, 20th April, 2017).

These results confirm the study of Vernon (1995) which revealed that PBL fosters student interaction, teamwork and reinforces interpersonal skills like peer evaluation, working with group dynamics as groups resolve relevant problems in collaboration. In addition, the results are in line with the findings of Vardi and Ciccarelli (2008) that employers have appreciated the positive attributes of communication, teamwork, respect and collaboration that PBL students have developed.

In relation to the statement that PBL develops students' confidence and attitude towards geography positively, majority of the student agreed to the statement and their responses were homogeneous (M= 4.49, SD= 0.73). Lastly, the result in Table 7 showed that majority of the respondents agreed that PBL helps students to identify their own deficiencies and progress through self-assessment and their responses did not differ much from one another. This is evident from the computed mean value of 4.42 and standard deviation value of 0.66. This finding did not differ from the responses from the focus group discussion. The students said this:

"PBL helps to clarify doubts or misconceptions held by some students. For example, discussion in problem based learning where every student brings out his opinion enables students to arrive at a proper understanding of issues at the end of the problem solving process and help clear any misconception held by any student prior to the discussion. Also, when the number of students in a group is not large, controlling the group will be much easier and everybody get involved in the task given. This teamwork in PBL is important because the explanations offered by colleague group members on a particular topic provide in-depth understanding. Since, students are involved in what they do, they tend to understand it more" (FGD B.Sc. Students, 21st April, 2017).

These findings are in harmony with the views of Havorson and Wescoat (2002) and Spronken-Smith (2005) who found that problem-based learning instruction in geography improve students' attitude positively towards geography. Likewise, other researchers (Dean, 1999; Lieux, 2001; Schmidt et al., 2006) have found PBL to be effective in enhancing students' confidence in judging alternatives for solving problems, acquiring social studies content to enrich their learning of basic science information among others. The overall responses on the benefits that result from the effective implementation of PBL method in geography had a mean and standard deviation values of the 4.60 and 0.61 respectively. The implication is that majority of the respondents strongly agreed that implementation of PBL method in geography education is very beneficial to students. These findings are very essential since education seeks to raise generations of problem solvers and positive agent of change in the society, the nation and world at large.

Summary of the Chapter

The chapter focused on the presentation and discussion of the findings from the study. It was divided into two sections namely the demographic data of the respondents and the discussion of main findings of the study. With respect to the demographics of the respondents, male students dominated the study. From the findings, it was revealed that, the instructors using PBL in teaching geography define the problem for students and specify the objectives and context in which a given problem should be solved or worked on. In addition, large class size, inadequate resources (time, material and financial), traditional assessment system among others were some of the challenges found to be affecting the effective implementation of PBL method in geography.

Furthermore, curriculum based on PBL ideas, and provision of support and guidance for students and instructors on the use of PBL method by the departments are some of the ways for ensuring effective implementation of PBL in geography. Besides, it was found that PBL develops geography students' observation and problem solving skills, confidence and attitude towards the subject, promotes lifelong learning among others. The next chapter is the summary, conclusions and recommendations made from the findings of the study.

CHAPTER FIVE

SUMMARY, CONCLUSIONS AND RECOMMENDATIONS

This chapter presents a summary of the study as well as the key findings that emerged from the research. The chapter also contains conclusions and recommendations that were made based on the findings of the study. Suggestions for future studies are also discussed under this chapter.

Summary of the Study

The study focused on investigating the efficacy of Problem-Based Learning Method in Geography Education in the University of Cape Coast. Specifically, the study sought to provide answers to four (4) research questions and two (2) hypotheses which were:

1. What are the processes or stages involved in the implementation of problem-based learning (PBL) in geography education?
2. What are the challenges affecting the effective implementation of PBL in geography?
3. What are the ways of ensuring effective implementation of PBL in geography?
4. What are the benefits of effective implementation of the PBL method in geography education?

The convergent parallel design under the mixed method research was the study design employed for the study. Since, the study employed both the quantitative and qualitative data collection techniques, convergent parallel design was adopted to determine how the quantitative and qualitative data converge. The target population for the study comprised all geography students and lecturers in the University of Cape Coast. The accessible population comprised Level 300 and 400 B.Sc. Geography and Regional Planning students and B.Ed. Social Sciences (Geography Major) students. The sample size for the study was 186 geography students which comprised both level 300 and 400 B.Sc. Geography and Regional Planning students and B.Ed. geography students. In addition to this, two lecturers were selected for in-depth interview whilst two focus group discussions comprising of eight (8) students each were also conducted.

A combination of census and purposive sampling techniques were employed. The census technique was used to involve the entire accessible population of the study (level 300 and 400 B.Sc. and B.Ed. geography students). This was due to the relatively smaller size of the accessible population. The two lecturers were purposively sampled for the interview on the grounds that they use PBL method in teaching their courses and as a result have specialized knowledge on the topic under study and for that matter could give the necessary information relevant to the study.

Questionnaire and interview guides were the research instruments employed to collect data from the geography students and lecturers in the two departments involved in the study. The questionnaire comprised a combination of close and open-ended questions which were administered on geography students. The close-ended items in the questionnaire were employed because the investigator aimed at ensuring uniformity in the responses provided by the students without any kind of subjectivity. The response choice for the closed-ended questions were constructed on five-point Likert scale as Strongly Agree=5, Agree=4, Not Sure=3; Disagree=2 and Strongly Disagree=1. The investigator used semi-structured type of interview guide to conduct in-depth interview for lecturers and focus group discussion for the geography student to allow flexibility and to enable probing for further questions that the questionnaire could not provide.

The responses from the questionnaire were coded and entered into SPSS computer software for analysis and interpretation. Descriptive statistical tools were employed in the analysis and the interpretation of the data. Frequencies and percentage counts were used in analysing the demographic information of the respondents' whist mean and standard deviation were used in analysing research questions one to four. Additionally, thematic analysis was employed to analyse the qualitative data.

Key Findings

Based on the analysed data and results, the following key findings were found.

1. Geography instructors define or present the problem-based learning problem to geography students to solve, specify the context in which the problem should be solved and guides them to form groups to work on a particular problem in PBL implementation process. In addition, the instructors guide students/groups to give regular reports on the problem-solving process and individually assume responsibility in the PBL implementation, as well as serving as facilitators in providing guidelines for students in PBL process in geography. Though, instructors organise brainstorming sessions with groups before students start solving a given problem and guides students/groups to evaluate their own learning in the PBL implementation, it was not always that the instructors do that.

2. Large class size and its difficulty in maintaining effective learning with large number of groups in class; loaded nature of the geography curriculum, traditional assessment (examination) system, conventional teaching method (lecture), inadequate logistics, time consuming and expensive nature of using the PBL method were some of the factors that were found to negatively affect

the effective implementation of Problem-based learning method in geography education.

3. Majority of the respondents strongly agreed that instructors should provide clear guidelines and explanation of what students should do in the PBL process (M= 4.59, SD= 0.561); assessment of students in PBL should focus on students' creativity and problem solving outcome, curriculum based on PBL ideas needs to be used by the department in teaching geography and time allocation for geography courses should be increased for effective implementation of PBL. Again, the respondents agreed that the department should provide support and guidance for students and instructors on the use of PBL method and instructors should hold class discussion with various groups of students before they start solving the problem given as well as students/groups should give regular report during the PBL implementation process.

4. Problem-Based Learning (PBL) in geography develops geography students' intellectual/critical thinking skills, observation and problem solving skills, promotes students' self-directed and life-long learning, nurtures the leadership qualities in students and reinforces student communication and interpersonal skills. Additionally, its promotes teamwork among geography student groups, develops geography students' confidence and attitude towards geography positively and also helps students to identify their own deficiencies and progress through self-assessment.

Conclusions

From the findings of this study, the following conclusions were made.

From the key findings of the research question one, it can be inferred that the geography instructors using PBL method in Workshop Planning and Methods of Teaching Geography go through the appropriate processes or stages in implementing the method in geography. Hence, they are effective in implementing PBL method in teaching geography courses.

With regards to the keys findings of the research question two, the investigator can conclude that large class size, traditional assessment system, inadequate resources, loaded nature of the geography curriculum among others are some of the factors affecting the effective implementation of the PBL method in teaching geography courses. Therefore, the full beauty and purpose of the use of PBL method may not be achieved if these limiting factors are not critically looked at.

Owing to the key findings of the research question three, it can be inferred that restructuring the geography curriculum to incorporate PBL goals and guidelines, providing clear guidelines and explanation of what students are expected to do, assessing students out of their acts of creativity and problem-solving self-management and teamwork as well as provision of supports and guidance from the department and administration would ensure effective implementation of PBL method in geography education. This would enhance the benefit of its implementation in geography education.

Based on the key findings of the research question four, the investigator can conclude that effective implementation of PBL method in geography education develops geography students critical thinking, observation, problem-solving skills, promotes students' life-long learning, nurtures the leadership qualities in students, reinforces student communication, interpersonal and team work skills.

Recommendations

Based on the findings of the study and the conclusions that have been drawn, the following recommendations are made to ensure effective implementation of Problem-based learning in geography education.

1. The instructors employing PBL in teaching courses should be encourage to continue by the Head of the Departments of Geography and Regional Planning (DGRP) and Department of Business and Social Sciences Education (DBSSE). Also the Departments should officially adopt problem-based learning method in teaching geography courses so that other lecturers within the departments would employ it in their instructional process since it helps students to appreciate their environment. In so doing, The DGRP and DBSSE should organise seminar or workshop on the use of PBL Method in teaching geography courses and its related benefits in order to encourage other geography instructors who do not use the method as a result of inadequate information to use it.

2. The departments (DGRP & DBSSE) should provide support in terms of resources (time, financial and logistics) and guidance to students and instructors to aid the effective implementation of PBL method in teaching geography. If possible, a fund should be set up for such purpose where students can be levied as part of their fees to promote the effective use of the method. Alternatively, the Department can also use their internally generated funds to support use of the PBL implementation process. This is because PBL methods at times demand students to travel out of their classroom or geographical location to different locations to explore a phenomenon or problem and get new knowledge and solutions.

3. The problem presented to students to solve by instructors using the method must be clearer and free from ambiguity for easy understanding. Thus, there should be clear guidelines and explanation to students about what they are

expected to do during the problem solving process. Also, enough time should be given to enable students do effective research on problems presented or questions given.

4. The instructors using PBL method in teaching should focus or adopt problem-based learning assessment system or format which is based on evaluating students'/groups creativity, self-management, teamwork, presentation skills, problem solving outcome among others, rather than the traditional assessment system (i.e. the paper and pen test or exams). This will help realise the benefit of the effectiveness of the PBL method by both students and Instructors.

Suggestions for Further Research

It must be emphasised that this study forms part of other similar researches conducted in different areas. Taking into consideration its limitations, the investigator wishes to suggest that further research be conducted on the following areas:

1. Comparative study of the effects/impact of Problem-Based Learning and lecture method on geography students' academic performance.
2. Assessing students' attitude towards the study of geography in problem-based learning environment.
3. Investigating assessment techniques employed in problem-based learning classroom.

REFERENCES

Ababio, B. T. (2007). The place of geography in the school curriculum. *Journal of Counselling, Education and Psychology, 1(1)*, 25-35.

Ababio, B. T. (2009). The effective geography teacher. *Ghana Journal of Education and Teaching (GHAJET)* 8(2), 24-28.

Ababio, B.T. (2012). *Ghana senior high school geography series: Teachers' manual book I.* Saarbruken, Germany: LAP Lambert Academic Publishing.

Alfieri, L., Brooks, P. J., Aldrich, & Tenenbaum, H. R. (2011). Does discovery based instruction enhance learning. *Journal of Education   Psychology. 1, 1-8.*

Allen, D. E., Duch, B. J., & Groh, S. E. (1996). The power of problem-based learning in teaching introductory science course. In L. Wilkerson, & W. H. Gijselaers (Eds.), *Bringing problem-based learning into higher education: Theory and practice* (pp. 43–52). San Francisco, CA: Jossey Bass.

Allen, D. E., Duch, B. J., Groh, S. E., Watson, G. B., & White, H. B. (n.d.). *Scaling up research-based education for undergraduates: Problem-based learning.* Retrieved from http://www.cur.org/publications/aire_raire/delaware.asp

Alliance for Childhood. (2000). *Fool's gold: A critical look at computers in childhood.* Retrieved from   http://www.allianceforchildhood.net/projects/ computers/computers_reports.htm

Amu, T. J., Kwao, S., Mensah, V., & Tengfah, T. (2012). *The role of fieldwork in the teaching and learning of geography in senior high schools in the Cape Coast metropolis.* Unpublished project work, University of Cape Coast.

Antepohl, W., & Herzig, S. (1999). Problem-based learning versus lecture-based learning in a course of basic pharmacology: A controlled, randomized study. *Medical Education, 33, 106–113.*

Arambula-Greenfield, T. (1996). Implementing problem-based learning in a college science class. *Journal of College Science Teaching, 26*(1).

Armstrong, E. G. (2008). A hybrid model of problem-based learning. In B. David, & F. Grahame (Eds.), *The challenge of problem-based learning.* (pp. 26- 32).   London: Routledge.

Ary, D., Jacobs, L. C., Razavieh, A., & Sorensen, C. (2006). *Introduction to research in education.* (7th ed.). Canada: Thomson Wansworth Publishers.

Aziz, A. A., Yusof, K., Udin, M., Latif, A., & Yatim, J. M. (2013). *Inculcating sustainable development among engineering students: Assessing the impact on knowledge and behaviour change.* Cambridge, UK: Cambridge University Press.

Baker, T., & White, S. (2003). The effects of G.I.S. on students' attitudes, self-efficacy, and achievement in middle school science classrooms. *Journal of Geography, 102*(6), 243-254.

Balım, A., G. (2009). The effects of discovery learning on students' success and inquiry learning skills. *Egitim Arastirmalari-Eurasian Journal of Educational Research, 35*, 1-20.

Barrett, T. (2005). Understanding problem-based learning. In T. Barrett, I. Mac Labhrainn & H. Fallon (Eds.), *Handbook of enquiry and problem-based learning* (pp. 14–25). Galway: CELT.

Barrows, H. S. (1996). Problem-based learning in medicine and beyond: A brief overview. *New Directions for Teaching and Learning, 68, 3–12.*

Barrows, H. S. (2000). *Problem-based learning applied to medical education.* Southern. Illinois, Springfield: Illinois University School of Medicine.

Barrows, H. S., & Tamblyn, R. M. (1980). Problem based learning: An Approach to Medical Education. *Springer Series on Medical Education, 1.*

Bednarz, S. (2004). Geographic information systems: A tool to support geography and environmental education? *GeoJournal, 60,* 191-199.

Bekoe, S. O. (2006). *Assessment and curriculum goals and objectives: Evaluation of the systematic impact of the SSCE on the senior high school social studies curriculum in Ghana.* Unpublished doctoral dissertation, Faculty of Education, University of Strathclyde.

Bell, J. (2008). *Doing your research project: A guide for first-time researchers in education and social sciences.* (4th ed.). Maidenhead: Open University Press.

Béneker, T., Sanders, R., Tani, S., Taylor, L., & van der Vaart, R. (2007). Teaching the geographies of urban areas: Views and visions. *International Research in Geographical and Environmental Education, 16*(3), 250-267.

Benson, S. (2003). *Hunting the snark: A 1uest for excellence in information systems.* Unpublished doctoral dissertation, Curtin University of Technology.

Bergman, F. E., & Renwick, H. E. (2008). *Introduction to geography: People, places and environment.* (4th ed.). New Jersey: Pearson Prentice Hall.

Bhanu, S. (2011). *Census and sampling method.* Retrieved from http://bhanusigdel. wordpress.com/2011/11/17census-and-sampling- method/

Bligh, D. (2000). *What's the point in discussion?* Portland-Oregon: Intellect Books.

Blumberg, B. (2000). Evaluating the evidence that problem-based learners are self-directed learners: A review of the literature. In D.H. Evensen & C.E. Hmelo, (Eds), *Problem-based learning: A research perspective on learning interactions*, Mahwah, NJ: Erlbaum.

Bok, D. (2006). *Our underachieving colleges: A candid look at how much   students learn and why they should be learning more.* Princeton, NJ: Princeton University Press.

Bonwell, C. C. (1998). *Active learning: Energizing the classroom.* Green Mountain Falls, CO: Active Learning Workshops.

Bork, L., Hemmer, K. I., & Czapek, L. (2012). *Educational standards in geography for the Intermediate School Certificate with sample   assignments.* U.S.A: National Academy Press.

Bowling, A. (2002). *Research methods in health.* Philadelphia: Open University Press

Brickell, G., & Herrington, J. (2006). Scaffolding learners in authentic, problem based elearning environments: The geography challenge. *Australasian Journal of Educational Technology, 22*(4), 531-547.

Briggs, S. (2015). *10 tips for effective problem-based learning: The ultimate instructional solution.* Retrieved from www.opencolleges.edu.au/informed/ *features/problem-based-learning/*

Bruner, J. S. (1966). Some elements of discovery. In L. S., Shulman & E. R. Keislar, (Eds.). *Learning by discovery: A critical appraisal.* Chicago: Rand   McNally.

Chakravathi, S., & Haleagrahara, N. (2010). An exploration of the strategic challenges of problem based learning (PBL) in medical education environment: A paradigm shifts from traditional lectures. *Indian Journal of Science and Technology, 3*(2),

Cheong, F. (2008). Using a problem-based learning approach to teach an intelligent systems course. *Journal of Information Technology Education, 7,* 47–60.

Chung, J. C. C., & Chow, S. M. K. (2004). Promoting student learning through a student-centered problem-based learning subject curriculum. *Innov. Educ. Teaching Int., 41*(2), 157–168.

Cohen, L., Manion, L., & Morrison, J. (2007). *Research methods in education.* (6th ed.). London: Routledge Taylor and Francis group.

Colliver, J. A. (2000). Effectiveness of problem-based learning curricula: Research and theory. *Acad. Med., 75*(3), 259–266.

Cotič, M., & Zuljan, M. V. (2009). Problem-based instruction in mathematics and its impact on the cognitive results of the students and on affective- motivational aspects. *Educational Studies, 35*(3), 297–310.

Craft, E. L., & Mack, L. G. (2001). Developing and implementing an integrated, problem-based engineering technology curriculum in an American technical college system. *Community College Journal of Research & Practice, 25(5/6), 425-439.*

Creswell, J. W. (2008). *Educational research: Planning, conducting and evaluating quantitative and qualitative research.* (3rd ed.). New Jersey: Pearson Education.

Dahlgren, M. A. (2003). PBL through the looking-glass: Comparing applications in computer engineering, psychology and physiotherapy, *Intl. J. Engr. Education, 19*(5), 672–681.

De Graaff, E., & Kolmos, A. (2003). Characteristics of problem-based learning. *Intl. J. Engr. Education, 19*(5), 657–662.

Dean, C. D. (1999). *Problem-based learning in teacher education.* Paper presented at the Annual Meeting of American Educational Research Association, Montreal, Quebec, April 19–23.

Denscombe, M. (2008). *The good research guide for small scale social research project.* (3rd ed.). Buckingham: Open University Press.

Dewey, J. (1997). *How we think.* Mineola, New York: Dover.

Dillman, D. A. (2000). *Mail and internet survey: The tailored design method.* (2nd ed.). New York: John Wiley Co.

Drennon, C. (2005). Teaching geographic information systems in a problem-based learning environment. *Journal of Geography in Higher Education, 29*(3), 385-402.

Duch, B. J. (2001). Writing problems for deeper understanding. In B. Duch, S. E. Groh, & D. E. Allen (Eds.), *The power of problem-based learning: A practical 'how to' for teaching undergraduate courses in any discipline,* (pp. 47–53). Sterling, VA: Stylus Publishing.

Duch, B. J., Groh, S., & Allen, D. E. (2001). *The power of problem-based learning: A practical how to for teaching undergraduate courses in any discipline.* (1st ed.). Sterling, VA: Stylus Publishing.

Duch, B., Groch, S., & Allen, D. (Eds.). (2001). *The power of problem-based learning.* (1st ed.). Sterling, VA: Stylus Publishing.

Edens, K. M. (2000). Preparing problem solvers for the 21st Century through problem-based learning. *College Teaching, 48(2), 55–60.*

Egidius, H. (1999). *Problembaserat Lärande-en introduktion för lärare och lärande.* Stockholm: Studentlitteratur.

Evenson, D. H., & Hmelo, C. E., Eds. (2000). *Problem-based learning: A research perspective on learning interactions.* Mahwah, NJ: Lawrence Erlbaum Associates.

Farrant, J. S. (1996). *Principles and practice of education.* Singapore: Longman Publication.

Felder, R.M., & Brent, R. (2005). Understanding student differences. J. *Engr. Education, 94*(1), 57–72.

Fraenkel, J. R., & Wallen, N. E. (2006). *How to design and evaluate research in education.* (6th ed.). New York: Palgrave Macmillan.

Gallagher, S. A. (1997). Problem-based learning: Where did it come from, what does it do, and where is it going? *J. Educ. Gifted, 20*(4), 332–362.

Gallagher, S. A., Stepien, W. J., & Rosenthal, H. (1992). The effects of problem-based learning on problem solving. *Gifted Child Quarterly, 36, 195–200.*

Gasser, K. W. (2011, June). Five ideas for 21st Century math classrooms. *American Secondary Education, 39*(3), *108–16.*

Genareo, R. V., & Lyons, R. (2015). *Problem-based learning: Six steps to design, implement, and assess.* Retrieved from www.facultyfocus.com › articles › instructionaldesign.

Gentry, E. (2000). *Creating Student-centered, problem-based classrooms.* Huntsville: University of Alabama in Huntsville.

Gijbels, D., Dochy, F. P., Van den Bossche, P., & Segers, M. (2005). Effects of problem-based learning: A meta-analysis from the angle of assessment. *Review of Educational Research*, *75*(1), 27–61.

Gijselaers, W. H. (1996). Connecting problem based practices with educational theory. In L. Wilkerson & W. H. Gijselaers (Eds.), *Bringing problem-based learning to higher education: Theory and practice* (pp. 13-21). San Francisco: Jossey-Bass.

Golightly, A., & Muniz, O. A. (2013). Are South African geography education students ready for problem-based learning? *Journal of Geography in Higher Education, 37*(3), 432–455.

Gravett, S. (2001). *Adult learning: Designing and implementing learning events. A dialogic approach.* Pretoria: Van Schaik.

Grimwade, D. (2000). The national geographic society's teaching geography project. *Journal of Geography, 92(3),* 121-124.

Harding, J. (2013). *Census.* Retrieved from http://srmo.sagepub.com/view.the - sage-dictionary-of-social-research-methods/n18.xml

Havorson, S., & Wescoat, J. (2002). Problem-based inquiry on world water problems in large undergraduate classes. *Journal of Geography, 101*(3), 91-102.

Hayford, C. L. (1992). *Social studies education. Introduction to education in Ghana.* Accra: Sedco Ltd.

Healey, M. (2005). Linking research and teaching to benefit student learning. *Journal of Geography in Higher Education, 29*(2), pp 183–201.

Heffron, S., & Downs, R. (Eds.). (2012). *Geography for life: National geography standards.* (2nd ed.). Washington D.C.: National Council for Geographic Education.

Helmke, A. (2009). *Unterrichtsqualitaet und lehrerprofessionalitaet. diagnose, evaluation unterrichtsqualitaet und lehrerprofessionalitaet.* Seelze. Retrieved May 6, 2013 from www.seelze.org.

Hmelo-Silver, C. E, & Barrows, H. S. (2006). Goals and strategies of a problem-based learning facilitator. *Interdisciplinary Journal of Problem-Based Learning, 1*(1), 21-39.

Hung, W. (2006a). The 3C3R model: A conceptual framework for designing problems in PBL. *Interdiscip. J. Problem Based Learn., 1*(1), 55–77.

Hung, W. (2006b). *A 9-step PBL problems designing process: Application of the 3C3R model.* Paper presented at the 2006 AERA Annual Meeting, San Francisco, CA., April 8–12.

Hung, W. (2011). Theory to reality: A few issues in implementing problem-based learning. *Educational Technology Research and Development, 59*(4), 529–552.

Hung, W., Jonassen, D. H., & Liu, R. (2008). *Problem-based learning: Handbook of research on educational communication and technology.* Mahwah, NJ: Earlbaum.

Johnson, R. B. (2014). *Mixed methods research design and analysis with validity: A primer.* USA: University of South Alabama.

Johnson, R. B., & Onwuegbuzie, A. J. (2004). Mixed methods research: A research paradigm whose time has come. *Educational Researcher, 33*(7), 14-26.

Johnstone, B. D. (2004). *Financing higher education: Cost-sharing in international perspective.* New York: McGraw-Hill.

Jones, B. D., Epler, C. M., Mokri, P., Bryant, L. H., & Paretti, M. C. (2013). The effects of a collaborative problem-based learning experience on students' motivation in engineering capstone courses. *Interdisciplinary Journal of Problem-Based Learning, 7*(2), 34-71.

Kattah, M. A. (2015). *Teacher effectiveness in teaching and learning of geography: A study of selected senior high schools in the Cape Coast Metropolis.* Unpublished project work, University of Cape Coast, Cape Coast.

Keeling, A. (2008). We are scholars: Using teamwork and problem-based learning in a Canadian regional geography course. *Mountain Rise, 4*(3), 1–13.

Keller, G. E. I. (2002). Using problem-based and active learning in an interdisciplinary science courses for non-science majors. *Journal of General Education, 51*(4), 272-281.

Kelly, M. (2014). *Lecture as a teaching method – pros and cons.* Retrieved from 712educators.about.com/.../p/lecture.htm.

Klein, P. (1995). Using Inquiry to enhance the learning and appreciation of geography. *Journal of Geography, 94*(2), 358-367.

Kumekpor, T. K. B. (2002). *Research methods and techniques of social research.* Accra: SonLife Printing and Services.

Kuruganti, U., Needham, T., & Zundel, P. (2012). Patterns and rates of learning in two problem-based learning courses using outcome based assessment and elaboration theory. *The Canadian Journal for the Scholarship of Teaching and Learning, 3*(1), 56-62.

Kusi, H. (2012). *Doing qualitative research: A guide for researchers.* Accra-Newtown: Emmpong Press.

LaMarca, N. (2011). *The likert scale: Advantages and disadvantages.* Retrieved from https://Psyc450.wordpress.com/2011/12/the-likert-scale-advantages-and-disadvantages

Lee, J. (1999). *Problem-based learning: A decision model for problem selection.* In Proceedings of Selected Research and Development Papers Presented at the National Convention of the Association for Educational Communications and Technology (AECT), Houston, TX, February 10–14.

Lieux, E. M. (2001). A skeptic's look at PBL. In B. Duch, S. E. Groh, & D. E. Allen (Eds.), *The power of problem-based learning: A practical 'how to' for teaching undergraduate courses in any discipline,* (pp. 223–235). Sterling, VA: Stylus Publishing.

Lim, L. A., & Lew, M. (2012). Does academic performance affect the challenges faced by students in their initial adaptation to a problem-based learning environment? *Reflections on Problem-Based Learning, 13,* 4-9.

Lohman, M. C., & Finkelstein, M. (1999). *Segmenting information in PBL cases to foster the development of problem solving skill, self-directedness, and technical knowledge.* Unpublished Manuscript. Florida State University/University of Iowa.

Loveless, T. (1998). The use and misuse of research in educational reform. In Ravitch, D. (Ed.), *Education Policy* (pp. 285-286) Washington, DC: rooking's Institution Press.

Luk, K. F. (2004). *Primary school teachers' perceptions of their experience in using ICT for project-based learning.* Hong Kong: University of Hong Kong.

Macdonald, R. (2005). Assessment strategies for enquiry and problem-based learning. In T. Barrett, I. Mac Labhrainn, & H. Fallon, *Handbook of enquiry & problem-based learning* (pp. 85-93). Sheffield: Galaway.

Major, C. H., & Palmer, B. (2001). Assessing the effectiveness of problem-based learning in higher education: Lessons from the literature. *Academic Exchange Quarterly, 5*(1), 65-69.

Mansor, A. N., Abdullah, N. O., Wahab, J. A., Rasul, M. S., Mohd-Nor, M. Y., Mohd-Nor N., & Raof, R. A. (2015). Managing problem-based learning: Challenges and solutions for educational practice. *Asian Social Science, 11*(4), 259-268.

Mansur, D. I., Kayastha, S. R., Makaju, R., & Dongo, M. (2012). Problem based learning in medical education. *Kathmandu Univ. Med Journal, 10*(4), 78-82.

Massa, N., Dischino, M., Donnelly, J., Hanes, F., & DeLaura, J., (2012). Problem-based learning in a pre-service technology and engineering education course. *American Society for Engineering Education, AC,* 2012-4035.

Matson, J. O. (2006). Misconceptions about the nature of science, inquiry- based instruction, and constructivism: Creating confusion in the science classroom, *Electronic Journal of Literacy through Science, 5*(6), 1-10.

Mayer, R. R. (2013). *How engineers learn: A study of problem-based learning in the engineering classroom and implications for course design.* Unpublished masters' dissertation. Graduate Faculty, Iowa State University.

McBer, H. (2000). *Research into teacher effectiveness: A model of teacher effectiveness.* Philadelphia: Temple University Press.

McBurney, D. H. (2007). *Research methods.* New York: Matrix Productions.

Mergendoller, J., Maxwell, N., & Bellisimo, Y. (2006). The effectiveness of problem-based instruction: A comparative study of instructional methods and student characteristics. *Interdisciplinary Journal of Problem-based Learning, 1*(2), 49-69.

Mitchell, J. (2009). Hazards education and academic standards in the Southeast United States. *International Research in Geographical and Environmental Education, 18*(2), 134-148.

Nasr, K. J., & Ramadan, B. H. (2008). Impact assessment of problem-based learning in an engineering science course. *Journal of STEM Education: Innovations & Research, 9*(3), 16-24.

National Research Council (2006). *Learning to think spatially.* Washington, D.C.: The National Academies Press.

Nconco, F. (2006). *A comparative study of leadership and management approaches in further education and training colleges.* Unpublished thesis, Nelson Mandela Metropolis University, South Africa.

Neville, A. J. (2009). Problem-based learning and medical education forty years on. *Medical Principles and Practice, 18(1), 1–9.*

Oliver, P. (2006). *Purposive sampling. The SAGE dictionary social   research methods.* London: SAGE Publication.

Omoro, B., & Nato, L. W. (2014). Determining methods used in teaching geography in   secondary schools in Rongo District, Kenya. *International Journal of Academic Research in Progressive Education and   Development, 3(1),* 2-13.

Otabil, K. E., Dufie, S. B., Tandoh, G., & Mensah-Damoah, E. (2014). *Factors affecting the teaching and learning of geography: A case study of the department of geography and regional planning, University of Cape Coast.* Unpublished project work, University of Cape Coast.

Owusu, M., & Asare-Danso, S. (2014). Teachers' use of life themes pedagogy in Christian religious studies: A survey of senior high schools in Brong Ahafo Region, Ghana. *International Journal of Humanities and Social Science, 4*(11). Retrieved from www.ijhssnet.com.

Padmavathy, R. D., & Mareesh, K. (2013). Effectiveness of problem-based learning in mathematics. *International Multidisciplinary e – Journal, 2,* 45-51.

Pagander, L., & Read, J. (2014) *Is problem-based learning (PBL) an effective teaching method? A study based on existing research.* Retrieved from www.diva-portal.org.

Patterson, M., Reeve, K., & Page, D. (2003). Integrating geographic information systems into the secondary curricula. *Journal of Geography, 102*(6), 275-281.

Pawson, E., Fournier, E., Haigh, M., Muniz, O., Trafford J., & Vajoczki, S. (2006). Problem-based learning in geography: Towards a critical assessment of its purposes, benefits and risks. *Journal of Geography in Higher Education, 30*(1), 103-116.

Pepper, C. (2009). Problem based learning in science. *Issues in Educational Research, 19*(2), 120-140.

Peters, J. A., & Amador, L. M. C. B. (2006). *The practice of problem-based learning: A guide to implementing PBL in the college classroom.* Bolton, Mass: Anker Pub. Co.

Piaget, J. (1972). *The psychology of the child.* New York: Basic Books.

Plano-Clark, V. L., & Creswell, J. W. (2008). *The mixed methods reader.* Thousand Oaks, CA: SAGE Publication.

Plano-Clark, V. L., & Creswell, J. W. (2011). *Designing and conducting mixed methods research.* (2nd ed.). Thousand Oaks, CA: SAGE Publication.

Poikela, E., & Poikela, S. (2005). *PBL in context: Bridging work and education.* Tampere: Tampere University Press.

Prince, M. J., & Felder, R. M. (2006). Inductive teaching and learning methods: Definitions, comparisons, and research bases. *J. Engr. Education, 95*(2), 123–138.

Quain, A. J. (2014). *Assessing students' attitudes towards geography in a problem-based learning environment.* Unpublished Master's thesis, School of Teaching and Learning, Illinois State University, Illinios.

Reithlingshoefer, S. J. (Ed). (1992). *The future of non-traditional/interdisciplinary programs: Margin or mainstream?* Selected Papers from the Tenth Annual Conference on Non-traditional and Interdisciplinary Programs, Virginia Beach, VA, 1-763.

Richard, P. (2014). *Samples versus census.* Retrieved from http://survey.event. com/blog.conducting-online-surveys/samples-versus-census

Rogers, T. (2014). *Overcoming implementation challenges with problem and project based learning in advanced technological education programs within community colleges.* Unpublished doctoral thesis, School of Education, Northeastern University.

Sanson-Fisher, R. W., & Lynagh, M. C. (2005). Problem-based learning: A dissemination success story? *Medical Journal of Australia, 183*(5), 258-60.

Savin-Baden, M. (2000). *Problem-based learning in higher education: Untold stories.* Buckingham, UK: Open University Press.

Savin-Baden, M. (2001). *The problem-based learning landscape: Planet.* (2nd ed.). Retrieved from http://www.gees.ac.uk/planet/p4/msb.pdf

Schmidt, H. G., & van der Molen, H. T. (2001). Self-reported competency ratings of graduates of a problem-based medical curriculum. *Acad. Med., 76*(5), 466–468.

Schmidt, H. G., Loyens, S. M. M., Van Gog, T., & Paas, F. (2007). Problem-based learning is compatible with human cognitive architecture: Commentary on Kirschner, Sweller, and Clark (2006). *Educational Psychologist, 42*(2), 91–97.

Schmidt, H. G., Rotgans, J. I., & Yew, E. H. J. (2011). The process of problem-based learning: What works and why. *Medical Education, 45,* 792-806.

Schmidt, H. G., Vermeulen, L., & van der Molen, H. T. (2006). Long-term effects of problem-based learning: A comparison of competencies acquired by graduates of a problem-based and a conventional medical school. *Med. Educ., 40*(6), 562–567.

Scholkmann, A., & Roters, B. (2009). *Measuring the effects of problem-based learning progress in the development of a scale to rate the acquisition of professional knowledge through PBL: ECER 2009, theory and evidence in European educational research.* Vienna, Austria: Technische University of Dortmund.

Şendag, S., & Ferhan-Odabasi, H. (2009). Effects of an online problem based learning course on content knowledge acquisition and critical thinking skills. *Computers & Education, 53,* 132–141.

Shin, E. (2006). Using geographic information system (GIS) to improve fourth graders' geographic content knowledge and map skills. *Journal of Geography, 105*(3), 109-120.

Singh, R. P., & Rana, G. (2004). *Teaching strategies.* New Delhi: APH Publishing Corp.

Spencer, J. A., & Jordan, R. K. (1999). Learner-centred approach in medical education. *British Medical Journal, 318,* 1280–1283.

Spronken-Smith, R. (2005). Implementing a problem-based learning approach for teaching research methods in geography. *Journal of Geography in Higher Education, 29*(2), 203-221.

Tai, G. X. L., & Yuen, M. C. (2007). *Authentic assessment strategies in problem-based learning: Providing choices for learners and learning.* Singapore: Proceedings ascilite, 983-993.

Tamakloe, E. K. (2004). *Preparing for teaching practice and process of teaching.* (3rd ed.). Cape Coast: Winx Computers.

Tamakloe, E. K., Atta, E. T., & Amedahe, F. K. (1996). *Principles and methods of teaching.* Accra: Black Mask Ltd.

Tan, O. S. (2003). *Problem-based learning innovation.* Singapore: Thomson.

Tricia, S., & Moore, R. D. H. (2007). Implementation of Problem-Based Learning in a Baccalaureate Dental Hygiene Program. *Journal of Dental Education,   71, 1058–1069.*

Tulloch, D., & Graff, E. (2007). Green map exercises as an avenue for problem-based learning in a data-rich environment. *Journal of Geography, 106*(6), 267-276.

Twumasi, P. A. (2001). *Social research in rural communities.* (2nd ed.). Accra: Ghana University Press.

Utecht, R. J. (2003). *Problem-based learning in the student centered classroom.* Retrieved from *www.jeffutecht.com/docs/PBL.pdf*

Vardi, I., & Ciccarelli, M. (2008). Overcoming problems in problem-based learning: A trial of strategies in an undergraduate unit. *Innovations in   Education   and Teaching International, 45*(4), 345–354.

Vernon, D. T. (1995). Attitudes and opinions of faculty tutors about problem-based learning. *Academic Medicine, 70,* 216–223.

Vernon, D. T., & Blake, R. L. (1993). Does problem-based learning work? A meta-analysis of evaluative research. *Academic Medicine, 68, 550–563.*

Vogler, K., & Virtue, D. (2007). Just the facts, ma'am: Teaching social studies in the era of standards and high-stakes testing. *The Social Studies, 98*(2), 54-58.

Vygotsky, L.S. (1978). *Mind in society.* Cambridge, MA: Harvard University Press.

Walker, S. (2006). Development and validation of the Test of Geography-Related Attitudes (ToGRA). *Journal of Geography, 105*(4), 175-181.

Waters, R., & McCracken, M. (1997). *Assessment and evaluation in problem-based learning.* Georgia: Georgia Institute of Technology.

Waugh, D. (2009). Geography: An integrated approach. Phenomenographic categories for common knowledge construction. *Geography Education, 85,* 509-535.

Wee, L. K. N. (2000). *Tried and tested: Issues & implications for educators in PBL Learning: Relearning from the learners; perspective post conference proceedings.* 2nd Asia Pacific Conference on PBL, Singapore, 4-7 December 2000.

Weiss, R. E. (2003). Designing problems to promote higher order thinking. In D.   S. Knowlton, & D. C. Sharp, (Eds.), *Problem-based learning in the   information age,* (pp. 25–31). San Francisco, CA: Jossey-Bass.

White, H. (2001). Problem-based learning. *Speaking for Teaching, 11*(1), 2-8.

Wilkerson, L., & Gijselaers, W. H. (1996). Editors' Notes. In L. Wilkerson, & H. Gilselaers (Eds.), *Bringing problem-based learning to higher education: Theory and practice* (pp. 1-9). San Franscisco, CA: Jossey-Bass Inc.

Wong, C. H., Wong, M. C., & Tang, S. L. (2011). *Examining the effectiveness of adopting an inductive approach to the teaching of English grammar.* Retrieved from http://www.edb.org.hk/HKTC/download/eras/1011/ER AS1011_R09.pdf

Woods, D. R. (1996). Problem-based learning for large classes in chemical engineering. In L. Wilkerson, & H. Gijselaers (Eds.), *Bringing problem-based learning to higher education: Theory and practice,* (pp. 91–99). San Francisco, CA: Jossey-Bass.

Wu, C. V., & Fournier, E. J. (2000). Coping with course content demands in a problem-based learning environment, *Journal of the Alabama Academy of Science, 71*(3), 110–119.

APPENDICES

APPENDIX A

UNIVERSITY OF CAPE COAST
FACULTY OF HUMANITIES AND SOCIAL SCIENCES EDUCATION

DEPARTMENT OF BUSINESS AND SOCIAL SCIENCES EDUCATIONTION

QUESTIONNAIRE FOR STUDENTS

Dear Participant,

I am a Master's student at the University of Cape Coast, who is undertaking a research project under the theme **"Assessing the Implementation of Problem-Based Learning (PBL) Method in Geography Education in the University of Cape Coast"**. This self-completion questionnaire aims to collect information on the processes involved in the use of PBL, challenges affecting its effective use and ways for ensuring it effective implementation as well as the benefits of it effective implementation. The research is purely for academic purpose hence the honest and sincere response you give will contribute a lot to the research.

Participation in this research is voluntary, and you are under no obligation to participate. Your identity would be kept secret and the confidentiality of your responses guaranteed, as your name will not appear in the research report. In any sort of report that might be published, no information will be used that would make it possible to identify you. Should you feel not to answer some questions or complete some parts of the questionnaire you can do so. I appreciate the time and effort you are offering.

If you have any question about this research, please feel free to talk to me in person or contact me on 0242854499 or email me at either samuelbentil899@gmail.com

Your rights as a Participant

This research has been reviewed and approved by the Institutional Review Board of University of Cape Coast (UCCIRB). If you have any questions about your rights as a research participant, you can contact the Administrator at the IRB Office between the hours of 8:00 a.m. and 4:30 p.m. through the phones lines 0332133172 and 0244207814 or email address: irb@ucc.edu.gh.

Section A: Demographic Data of Respondents

Please tick [√] appropriately: and write where necessary.

1. Name of Department: ....
2. Programme Pursued: ....
3. Class Level (Year Group) ....
4. Gender: Male [   ]   Female [   ]

93

Instructions:

For the following items, please read carefully and select the response which best expresses your experience about each statement by ticking ($\sqrt{}$) the appropriate box. Indicate the extent to which you agree or disagree to the statements in Section B to E, from question numbers 5 to 30, using the guide below:

- Strongly Agree **(SA) – 5:** To a large extent, you do accept the statement as it applies to students' estimation of efficacy of PBL.
- Agree **(A) - 4:** To some extent, you do accept the statement as it applies to students' estimation of efficacy of PBL.
- Not Sure **(NS) – 3:** You are uncertain as to whether you agree or do not agree with the statement.
- Disagree **(D) – 2:** To some extent, you do NOT accept the statement as it applies to students' estimation of efficacy of PBL.
- Strongly Disagree **(SD) – 1:** To a large extent, you do NOT accept the statement as it applies to students' estimation of efficacy of PBL.

Section B: Processes or Stages Involved in PBL Implementation in Geography

No.	Statement	SA	A	NS	D	SD
	Preamble: The instructor………………..					
5.	Defines or presents the PBL problem to students to solve.					
6.	Specifies the context in which the problem should be solved.					
7.	Guides students' to form groups to work on a particular problem in PBL implementation process.					
8.	Organises brainstorming sessions with groups before students start solving the problem.					
9.	Guides students/groups to give regular reports on the problem solving process.					
10.	Serves as a facilitators providing guidelines for students in the PBL process.					
11.	Guides students to individually assume responsibility in the PBL implementation					

	process.					
12.	Guides students/groups to evaluate their own learning in the PBL implementation process.					

Section C: Challenges Affecting the Effective Implementation of PBL in Geography

No.	Statement	SA	A	NS	D	SD
13.	Large class size negatively affects the use of PBL in geography.					
14.	Instructors have difficulty in maintaining the effectiveness of learning with large numbers of groups in a class.					
15.	The loaded nature of the geography curriculum makes it difficult to use PBL method in teaching.					
16.	The traditional assessment (examination) system affects the use of PBL in geography.					
17.	PBL method is time consuming and that makes it difficult to be used effectively in geography.					
18.	Inadequate logistics affects effective use of PBL method in geography.					
19.	The expensive nature of the PBL method makes it difficult to be implemented effectively.					
20.	The conventional teaching method (Lecture) where students look up to the instructor for knowledge affects the use of PBL.					

Section D: Ways of Ensuring Effective Implementation of PBL in Geography

No.	Statement	SA	A	NS	D	SD
21.	Curriculum based on PBL ideas needs to be used by the department.					
22.	Time allocation for geography courses should be increased for effective implementation of PBL.					
23.	The department should provide support and guidance for students and instructors on the use of PBL method.					
24.	Regular reports should be given by students during the PBL implementation process.					
25.	Instructors should provide clear guidelines and explanation of what students should do in the PBL process.					
26.	Instructors should hold class discussion with various groups of students before they start solving the problem given them.					
27.	Assessment of students in PBL should focus on students' creativity and problem solving outcome.					

Section E: Benefits of Effective Implementation of PBL in Geography

No.	Statement	SA	A	NS	D	SD
	Preamble: PBL………………					
28.	Develops student intellectual/critical thinking skills.					
29.	Develops student observation and problem solving skills.					
30.	Promotes students' self-directed and life-long learning.					
31.	Nurtures the leadership qualities in students.					
32.	Reinforces student communication and interpersonal skills.					
33.	Promotes teamwork among students' groups.					
34.	Develops students' confidence and attitude towards geography positively.					
35.	Helps students to identify their own deficiencies and progress through self-assessment.					

APPENDIX B

UNIVERSITY OF CAPE COAST

FACULTY OF HUMANITIES AND SOCIAL SCIENCES EDUCATION

DEPARTMENT OF BUSINESS AND SOCIAL SCIENCES EDUCATIONTION

PROTOCOL FOR FOCUS GROUP DISCUSSION

Dear Participants'

Thank you for voluntarily agreeing to participate in this interview regarding the efficacy of problem-based learning method in geography education in the University of Cape Coast. From your voluntary participation I will be able to derive data that will elucidate if problem-based learning is efficacious in geography education in the University of Cape Coast.

1. What are some of the processes or stages that you go through when using PBL as a method of instruction in geography?

2. Does your lecturer define the objective and the context in which the problem should be solved? Yes [ ]   No[ ]

3. Do you form groups each time you use PBL method in geography? Yes [ ] No [ ]

4. If yes, how many students form a group?

5. Is it the lecturer who presents the ill-structured problem to be solved by you or you come up with a problem and explore to solve?

6. Do you, individually or collaboratively assume responsibility for generating learning issues?

7. What are some of the problems that affect the effective implementation of the PBL method in geography?

8. How does the traditional assessment system affect the use of PBL in geography courses?

9. In what ways can problem-based learning method be implemented effectively in geography education?

10. What are some of the benefits you have gotten from the use of PBL as a method for geography instructions by your lecturer?

11. Do you prefer PBL method for teaching geography to Lecture method?

    Yes [ ]   No[ ]

12. If yes, why?

APPENDIX C

UNIVERSITY OF CAPE COAST
FACULTY OF HUMANITIES AND SOCIAL SCIENCES EDUCATION

**DEPARTMENT OF BUSINESS AND SOCIAL SCIENCES
EDUCATIONTION**

INTERVIEW GUIDE FOR LECTURERS' INTERVIEW

1. What are some of the processes or stages that you go through when using PBL as a method of instruction in geography?

2. What are some of the difficulties do you encounter in the implementation of PBL method in geography?

3. Does the large class size problem in PBL implantation process contributes to truancy of some students in the class? Yes [ ]   No[ ]

4. If yes, how does it contribute to that?

5. How does the traditional assessment system affect the use of PBL in geography courses?

6. How does students' orientation about the conventional method of teaching tertiary students affect the implementation of PBL method?

7. In what ways can problem-based learning method be implemented effectively in geography education?

8. Do you see PBL method to be beneficial to your geography students?
   Yes [ ]   No[ ]

9. If yes, how is it beneficial to your students?

10. Do you suggest problem-based learning method should be used in teaching geography courses? Yes [ ]   No [ ]

11. If yes, why should it be used in teaching geography courses?